SPECIAL EDUCATION AND SCHOOL NURSES

A MANUAL FOR PRACTITIONERS WHO WORK WITH STUDENTS IN SPECIAL EDUCATION

SPECIAL EDUCATION AND SCHOOL NURSES

FROM ASSESSMENTS TO IEPS

Frances Belmonte-Mann, MA, BSN, RN, IL PEL/School Nurse, IL PEL/ADM, NCSN
with
Jessica H. Gerdes, MS, BSN, RN, IL PEL/School Nurse, NCSN

SPECIAL EDUCATION AND SCHOOL NURSES
FROM ASSESSMENTS TO IEPS

iUniverse books may be ordered through booksellers or by contacting:

iUniverse
1663 Liberty Drive
Bloomington, IN 47403
www.iuniverse.com
1-800-Authors (1-800-288-4677)

ISBN: 978-1-5320-7743-2 (sc)
ISBN: 978-1-5320-7744-9 (e)

Print information available on the last page.

iUniverse rev. date: 07/25/2019

This book is dedicated first to our dear spouses, Mark H. Mann and Dean L. Gerdes, who patiently supported us as we spent many an evening and weekend away from family activities.

We also dedicate this book to our parents, Louise and Albert "McGee" Belmonte, Evelyn and Myron Mann, and Boni and Ed Hanchar, who raised daughters to believe they could make the world a better place.

You can't educate a child who isn't healthy,
and you can't keep a child healthy who isn't educated.

—Joycelyn Elders, MD, former surgeon general of the United States

CONTENTS

Section 1
Background and Foundation of Special Education

Section 2
The Special Education Process

Section 3
The Special Education Meeting

FOREWORD

This book is a must-read for all school nurses who work with students with special needs. As an increasing number of students are entering our schools with complex medical needs, the role of the school nurse is critical. Teachers, administrators, and other school personnel need the support of the school nurse. Parents and students with varied medical needs rely on the expertise of school nurses and find comfort in the fact that school nurses are dedicated to their needs.

The authors bring a wealth of expertise to the field of school nursing having served in the schools daily for many years. They understand the challenges that are faced every day, and they share their real-life experiences in this book, which will be a classic for all who serve students with medical needs in school.

In whatever role we serve, we should all have a thorough understanding of the important role of the school nurse. This book provides that needed resource.

—Beverley Holden Johns, MS, Special Education
Chair, Illinois Special Education Coalition

PREFACE

This book is a collaboration between a current school nurse and former nursing instructor and a former school nurse consultant at a state board of education.

They came together to write this book when Frances Belmonte-Mann was searching for a concise text on the school nurse's role in special education assessment, planning, and evaluation for a student and found many references in multiple texts, websites, and documents but no single source that pulled it all together. She sought the resources of the state education department, and that's when she met Jessica Gerdes.

The Illinois State Board of Education has as most states have adopted rules to inform school administrators and others of the requirements for completing the assessment, planning, and evaluation of special education students, but, similar to other state education departments, it offered no clear direction for the school nurse's function.

The authors conceived and wrote this book based on the need they discovered. They hope you find this book the resource they had been looking for years ago.

ACKNOWLEDGMENTS

We express our deepest gratitude to all the parents and exceptional children who have touched our lives and who have inspired us to write this book on special education.

We believe it is very important for school nurses and administrators to understand the role of the school nurse in the special education process in public schools. We acknowledge all the school administrators and special education department personnel who always welcomed us to be very active contributing members of their special education teams.

We especially want to thank the other school nurses who throughout the years with their encouragement led us to write this book. We can finally say, "It is finished!"

We extend our deepest and loving appreciation to our husbands and families for their encouragement and support in writing this book.

—Frances Belmonte-Mann
—Jessica Hanchar Gerdes

INTRODUCTION

Practicing school nurses have noticed a rise in recent years in the number of students with special needs and particularly in chronic conditions that affect education. School nurses new to the profession as well as more-experienced school nurses commonly seek each other's advice and guidance to help them navigate this new territory.

We wrote this book to provide that personal guidance in an easy-to-read, practical guide. It goes beyond the common health history to guide readers into implementing a full, comprehensive role in evaluating students' health—its strengths and limitations—as it relates to their academic achievement.

This guide teaches the school nurse to turn over every stone in a search for unknown health conditions or unrecognized effects of known health conditions. Both authors have discovered students' health conditions that had been minimized if not overlooked entirely.

This book will help school nurses and others understand the role school nurses play in the special education process and increase their knowledge in writing students' individualized education program (IEP) goals for health issues that affect students' learning.

This will be a meaningful guide for school staff members including principals, assistant principals, deans, department chairs, team leaders, special education coordinators, district administrators, and others responsible for managing aspects of schools as well as classroom teachers and others with questions about the role of the school nurse in special education.

The primary role of the school nurse in an IEP is to plan for nursing and academic services for students (from preschoolers through adolescents and young adults to age twenty-one) who have serious health conditions that may affect, or impact, their learning. This book will explain the importance of special education laws and the responsibility of school nurses to provide nursing services to students so they can succeed academically.

While the authors practice in Illinois, the information in this book can be applied to other states and US territories as most of the information and guidance is based on federal law and best practices. Because laws are always changing, it is best to check US Department of Education websites, such as www.ed.gov/idea/, and state departments of education websites for any laws or regulations that may have been implemented or updated.

This book is the first to address the health needs of students in public schools[1] written by an experienced school nurse consultant with state-level experience in two states and an expert former school nurse administrator in a large urban school district. They have served as adjunct professors or clinical instructors in university-level school nursing certification programs.

Each chapter contains steps that should be read consecutively beginning with the history of special education and the scaffolding with each step toward the conclusion—evaluating written IEP goals for students. Most of the language of special education and school nursing is explained throughout the chapters, and a comprehensive glossary at the end of the book offers a quick, easy reference to it.

This book affirms the science of nursing and provides many references to laws, rules, regulations, and evidence-based practices (EBPs). It offers instructional techniques and nursing interventions that research has shown to be most likely to improve student outcomes in a meaningful way. School nurses must also incorporate the art of nursing and creatively design care for the individual.

Florence Nightingale wrote,

> Nursing is an Art: and if it is made an art, it requires an exclusive devotion, as hard a preparation as any painter's or sculptor's work, for what is the having to do with dead canvas or dead marble, compared with having to do with the living body, the temple of God's spirit? It is one of the Fine Arts; I had almost said, the finest of Fine Arts. (AZquotes.com, 2019)

---

[1] Since private schools are not covered by federal special education laws, the nurse who works in a private school should contact the office of the public school district in which the private school is located to learn more about what, if any, responsibilities the private school has in provision of services for students with special needs.

SECTION 1

Background and Foundation of Special Education

CHAPTER 1

The School Nurse and Special Education

How did school nursing get its start? Since the early 1900s, school nurses have played a significant role in the health and well-being of children in public schools throughout the nation. It started in 1902 when Lillian Wald, a nurse activist, encouraged the New York City school system to provide school nursing services to increase attendance and improve health conditions of students in the city's public schools.

As described in the book *The House on Henry Street* (JWA.org, referencing the book by Lillian Wald, *The House on Henry Street*, New York: Henry Holt, 1915, 121), Wald's enthusiasm for the project "came from a deep-lying principle that every human being merits respectful consideration of his rights and his personality" (JWA.org, 2019). She was dedicated to the ideas that public schools must accommodate the needs of all their students and that all children deserve access to adequate health care and nutrition.

In 1902, Wald convinced Lina Rogers, a public health nurse who worked out of the community center known as the House on Henry Street, to work as New York City's first public school nurse with the goal of improving student attendance. In her first month, Lina Rogers treated 893 students referred to her by schools across the city, made 137 home visits related to those student encounters, and helped twenty-five students with severe medical issues who had received no prior medical attention (JWA.org, 2019). Those twenty-five students recovered and returned to school.

Impressed by her success, the New York Board of Health soon hired twelve school nurses to provide similar nursing services to the children in public schools to improve their health conditions and remain in school. Who knows how many of those students who were healed by the effort of Rogers and those who followed her went on to successful careers due to their efforts.

The role of the school nurse took on added significant in the years since Wald pioneered the role in New York City. Children began to receive new, complex treatments for diseases and conditions that in the past might not have allowed them to live to school age, and thus the demand for nursing services in schools grew.

Lillian Wald
Lillian Wald in a nurse's uniform, 1893. Used with permission,
courtesy of the Visiting Nurse Service of New York.

It is a great testimonial and accomplishment that school nurses have been involved with children in public schools since the turn of the century. Currently, nurses are in public schools, private schools, and charter schools throughout the nation to provide the best health care and maintain the well-being of students. This accomplishment reflects the passion and professionalism of school nurses past and present.

Current Special Education Data

The Individuals with Disabilities Education Act (IDEA), enacted in 1975, mandates that children and youth ages three to twenty-one with disabilities receive free and appropriate public school educations. According to the US Department of Education, National Center for Education Statistics *Digest of Education Statistics*, the percentage of total public school enrollment that represents children served by federally supported special education programs increased from 8.3 percent to 13.8 percent between school year 1976–77 and school year 2004–05 (US Department of Education, 71).

Today, most experienced school nurses have noticed an increased number of children with IEPs with increased medical needs requiring special education services and nursing services that may be provided only by nurses—registered nurses, licensed practical nurses, or licensed vocational nurses—according to each state's laws on the scope of nursing practices. The *Digest of Education Statistics* reported that by 2013–14, the number of students served under IDEA was 6.5 million, 13 percent of total public school enrollment (US Department of Education, 827).

In the same *Digest of Education Statistics* report, we read,

> However, there were different patterns of change in the percentages served with some specific conditions between 2004–05 and 2014–15. The percentage of children identified as having other health impairments, [OHI], limited strength, vitality, or alertness due to chronic or acute health problems such as a heart condition, tuberculosis, rheumatic fever, nephritis, asthma, sickle cell anemia, hemophilia, epilepsy, lead poisoning, leukemia, or diabetes, rose from 1.1 to 1.7 percent of total public school enrollment; the percentage with autism rose from 0.4 to 1.1 percent, and the percentage with developmental delay rose from 0.7 to 0.8 percent. (US Department of Education, 71–72)

Throughout the United States, school districts are increasingly confronted with requests to provide educational programs for students with special health care needs. It is important for school districts to provide medically safe and educationally sound programs for students with health care needs. The health care needs of a student may be chronic or acute, mild or medically fragile; students may have complex and risky health conditions requiring constant professional nursing care; and some may require highly technical equipment. School nurses, the professional team, and parents must work together to address the health needs or concerns of students who have chronic illnesses or other disabilities and require individualized IEPs.

CHAPTER 2

History of Special Education

The history of identifying learning disabilities to create special education programs started in a meeting in 1963 in Chicago with a group of very concerned parents and educators. At this first meeting, the group under the leadership of Samuel Kirk discussed children with various learning problems struggling in school due to various neurological problems.

The group agreed to use a single term, learning disability (LD), to identify all children who required extra educational instruction in the belief it best described children with special instructional needs. This term was adopted widely by all concerned and is still used today. In current terms, a learning disability is defined more specifically as dysfunction in processing information typically found in language-based activities that interferes with someone's learning how to read and write, do math, or both.

The group that coined the term developed into a new association called Learning Disabilities of America (LDA). As of this publication, the

> LDA headquarters continue to be located in Pittsburgh, where a staff supports the nationwide work of hundreds of key volunteer leaders, an annual conference that draws upward of 3000 participants annually, and answer hundreds of queries from individuals, families and professionals every day. (Learning Disabilities of America, n.d. "About Us: History of LDA." Accessed October 16, 2018. https://ldaamerica.org/about-us/history/)

Special Education Law[2]

The most accepted definition of learning disabilities first appeared in a 1975 federal law known as the Public Law 94–142, the Education for All Handicapped Children Act (EHCA) to support children with "unique educational needs" in school. Prior to the 1970s, students with disabilities often did not attend school or lived in boarding schools or other institutions for students with disabilities. Many students in those decades exhibited symptoms of significant intellectual disabilities similar to those the character in the book and movie *Forrest Gump* had. He as did countless others like him had a mother who "thought it would be good for me to go to the public school cause maybe it would hep [sic] me to be like everybody else" but, like others, "they come an [sic] told Mam I ought'n to be in there with everybody else" and "they put me in another sor of school" (Groom 1986, 4).

In first-person narrative, Forrest described that school as a place where they finger painted, learned to tie shoes and "not slobber" but "no book learnin [sic] to speak of" (Groom, 4). Self-aware, he said, "I think it was for the purpose of keepin [sic] us out of everybody else's hair" (Groom, 5). He said,

> I'm probably a lot brighter than folks think, cause what goes on in my mind is a sight different than what folks see. For instance, I can *think* things pretty good, but when I got to try sayin [sic] or writin [sic] them, it kinda come out like jello or somethin [sic]. (Groom, 2)

More recently, a young man named Dannell P. Malloy was considered "mentally retarded" until he was diagnosed with dyslexia. He went on to become governor of Connecticut. His full story is described in more detail in "Dyslexic Governor Brings Learning Disabilities to Limelight" (Reitz 2011).

The law has evolved over the years, but the key purpose of special education for students has remained unchanged since this first mandate in 1975: to allow students with disabilities to receive an education and training for successful futures. Prior to 1975, students with significant disabilities were often placed in institutions partially or fully or remained at home due to the inability or unwillingness of schools to accommodate their disabilities so they could fully participate in school.

Occasionally, students with minor disabilities or high-functioning disabilities were mainstreamed into school settings, but such integration was at times not welcomed by parents of students without disabilities. The law was significant in that for the first time, federal law supported the desire of parents of children with disabilities for their children to attend school and receive an education

---

[2] References to "law" or "legal" issues are sourced or are mentioned as part of the authors' education and experience related to nursing or education law and are not meant to reflect the opinions or knowledge of practicing attorneys in either nursing, medicine, or education.

appropriate to their disabilities along with their normally developing peers. If Stephen Hawking had exhibited his disability in childhood, is it possible that his intellect would have been left to fallow and never mature?

In 1990, EHCA was first revised and became the Individuals with Disabilities Education Act (IDEA). In 1997, IDEA was expanded to include two new federal programs for young children from birth to age three: early intervention services (EIS), a program that provides supports and services for families to help their children under age three meet developmental milestones, and Child Find, a legal requirement that schools find all children with disabilities who may be entitled to special education services.

While EIS covers children under age three, Child Find is a concept that includes all children from birth to age twenty-one who may have disabilities, may be at risk for future educational difficulties, and may be entitled to special education services. Many school districts find the children through screening programs open to the public and through referrals from health departments, nongovernmental agencies, or parents who call schools based on referrals from their primary care doctors or other sources. The school must evaluate any child presented to it with known or suspected disabilities by screening current students and inviting parents to bring preschoolers to the school for screening. The process of Child Find usually begins with formal screening programs using various tools and/or assessments to rule out or determine eligibility for special education services in the public school.[3]

Once a child is referred and found eligible for these services, the early intervention (EIS) team and parents will develop an individualized family service plan (IFSP), a plan similar to an IEP but written for children under age three. After a child turns two years and ten months old, the district will initiate another evaluation known as a full case study evaluation (CSE) to analyze the child's abilities as well as skills to link the cause and the result of any identified disabilities if possible. This CSE is conducted at the children's home school or district to determine if they are still eligible for special education and related services provided by specialized instructional support personnel (SISP) such as nursing, physical therapy (PT), occupational therapy (OT), and speech therapy.

Child Find is a defined process, but it is also a part of the art of nursing. These examples show how the art of nursing benefits children:

1. A school nurse may have a student who has been newly diagnosed with leukemia, diabetes, or other acute health condition that often becomes chronic and may find for the student whether additional education accommodations need to be made. If so, she or he refers the

[3] Child Find may also discover children who have characteristics that may put them at risk for school failure but without specific identified disabilities. School districts often have at-risk preschools, referrals to Head Start, or other programs to assist these children.

student for a special education evaluation to detect fine deficits in the student's ability to learn due to chemotherapy, radiation, or other treatments and advocates for the student.

2. A school nurse may conduct a routine vision screening that results in a failure and referral for further examination. A kindergarten physical examination might determine a child might have congenital cataracts that the parent said were pinpoint and were not affecting the child's ability to see. When large cataracts requiring surgery are discovered, the nurse may refer the child for further evaluation to determine if the duration of the condition has affected the child's academics and refer the child for special education services.
3. Another student was referred to the nurse for sleeping in class, and the student reported that he had no idea why he was occasionally sleeping (about once a week) in class, nor did he remember what occurred prior to the sleeping episode. The nurse referred the child for a workup, and the child was diagnosed with petit mal seizures. Since the student was also struggling academically, he was referred for special education evaluation.
4. Yet another student was discovered to have marks on his forearm that could have been caused by insect or human bites or self-inflicted; that might indicate a behavioral issue. The child was later diagnosed with autism and referred for special education evaluation.

Child Find does not exclude students who are not readily known to need educational accommodations; rather, it finds, identifies, refers, and advocates for students who may need such accommodations.

In 2004, IDEA was again revised and expanded and was reauthorized as the Individuals with Disabilities Education Improvement Act. In December 2015, it was amended again and became the Every Student Succeeds Act (ESSA). For the purposes of this book, we will simply refer to federal special education law as IDEA with the understanding that we mean the latest version of the federal law on disabilities and education.

IDEA Law

IDEA grants eligible students with disabilities the legal right to receive a free and appropriate public education (FAPE), an educational right of disabled children guaranteed by the Rehabilitation Act of 1973 and the IDEA in the least restrictive environment (LRE), meaning the school setting that minimizes their exclusion from their nondisabled peers.

Thirteen types of disabilities in the IDEA as written in the Code of Federal Regulations, Education, Section 300.8, are listed below and in appendix 1.

1. Autism means a developmental disability significantly affecting verbal and nonverbal communication and social interaction generally evident before age three that adversely

affects a child's educational performance. Other characteristics often associated with autism are engagement in repetitive activities and stereotyped movements, resistance to environmental change or change in daily routines, and unusual responses to sensory experiences.

2. Deaf-blindness means concomitant hearing and visual impairments, the combination of which causes such severe communication and other developmental and educational needs that they cannot be accommodated in special education programs solely for children with deafness or children with blindness.
3. Deafness means a hearing impairment that is so severe that the child is impaired in processing linguistic information through hearing with or without amplification that adversely affects a child's educational performance.
4. (i) Emotional disturbance means a condition exhibiting one or more of the following characteristics over a long period of time and to a marked degree that adversely affects a child's educational performance.

   (A) An inability to learn that cannot be explained by intellectual, sensory, or health factors.
   (B) An inability to build or maintain satisfactory interpersonal relationships with peers and teachers.
   (C) Inappropriate behavior or feelings under normal circumstances.
   (D) A general pervasive mood of unhappiness or depression.
   (E) A tendency to develop physical symptoms or fears associated with personal or school problems.

   (ii) Emotional disturbance includes schizophrenia. The term does not apply to children who are socially maladjusted unless it is determined that they have an emotional disturbance under paragraph (c)(4)(i) of this section.

5. Hearing impairment means an impairment in hearing whether permanent or fluctuating that adversely affects a child's educational performance but that is not included under the definition of deafness in this section.
6. Intellectual disability means significantly below-average general intellectual functioning, existing concurrently with deficits in adaptive behavior and manifested during the developmental period, that adversely affects a child's educational performance. The term *intellectual disability* was formerly termed *mental retardation*.
7. Multiple disabilities means concomitant impairments (such as intellectual disability-blindness or intellectual disability-orthopedic impairment), the combination of which causes such severe educational needs that they cannot be accommodated in special

education programs solely for one of the impairments. Multiple disabilities does not include deaf-blindness.

8. Orthopedic impairment means a severe orthopedic impairment that adversely affects a child's educational performance. The term includes impairments caused by a congenital anomaly, impairments caused by disease (e.g., poliomyelitis, bone tuberculosis), and impairments from other causes (e.g., cerebral palsy, amputations, and fractures or burns that cause contractures).
9. Other health impairment means having limited strength, vitality, or alertness, including a heightened alertness to environmental stimuli, that results in limited alertness with respect to the educational environment, that

   (i) Is due to chronic or acute health problems such as asthma, attention deficit disorder or attention deficit hyperactivity disorder, diabetes, epilepsy, a heart condition, hemophilia, lead poisoning, leukemia, nephritis, rheumatic fever, sickle cell anemia, and Tourette's syndrome; and
   (ii) Adversely affects a child's educational performance.

10. Specific learning disability—

    (i) General. Specific learning disability means a disorder in one or more of the basic psychological processes involved in understanding or in using language, spoken or written, that may manifest itself in the imperfect ability to listen, think, speak, read, write, spell, or to do mathematical calculations, including conditions such as perceptual disabilities, brain injury, minimal brain dysfunction, dyslexia, and developmental aphasia.
    (ii) Disorders not included. Specific learning disability does not include learning problems that are primarily the result of visual, hearing, or motor disabilities, of intellectual disability, of emotional disturbance, or of environmental, cultural, or economic disadvantage.

11. Speech or language impairment means a communication disorder, such as stuttering, impaired articulation, a language impairment, or a voice impairment, that adversely affects a child's educational performance.
12. Traumatic brain injury means an acquired injury to the brain caused by an external physical force, resulting in total or partial functional disability or psychosocial impairment, or both, that adversely affects a child's educational performance. Traumatic brain injury applies to open or closed head injuries resulting in impairments in one or more areas, such as cognition; language; memory; attention; reasoning; abstract thinking; judgment;

problem-solving; sensory, perceptual, and motor abilities; psychosocial behavior; physical functions; information processing; and speech. Traumatic brain injury does not apply to brain injuries that are congenital or degenerative, or to brain injuries induced by birth trauma.

13. Visual impairment including blindness means an impairment in vision that, even with correction, adversely affects a child's educational performance. The term includes both partial sight and blindness. (US Department of Education, Washington, DC, n.d., IDEA Individuals with Disabilities Act, Section 300.8, https://sites.ed.gov/idea/regs/b/a/300.8/a, accessed March 30 2019)

It is important to note that the definition of specific learning disability (SLD) does not include learning problems that are primarily the result of visual, hearing, or motor disabilities or of mental retardation, emotional disturbance (ED), or environmental, cultural, or physical development and health or economic disadvantages. This distinction leads to the school nurse's primary role in distinguishing within the category of specific learning disabilities.

For children under age ten, an additional eligibility category may include developmental delay (DD). Children from ages three through nine who are identified and receive these services under DD are not labeled as having a specific disability under the IDEA but are in the special category of DD. States have the option to limit the category to a subcategory of ages such as between three and six for placement.

The disabilities listed among the thirteen disabilities as well as DD must result in an adverse effect that affects a student's educational performance that requires specific special instruction and related services to support and benefit the child to be successful in school. The child may need related or support services such as school nursing or a session with a social worker to benefit from special education.

IDEA requires public schools to provide related services to students with disabilities if they are needed for the students to be successful with the special education program in school. The related service may be in or outside the classroom depending on the unique needs of the student.

Consider a student with an IEP for a learning disability (LD) who also has type 1 diabetes. The student was making progress until high school, when she assumed self-care for her diabetes. The nurse met with her to go over her self-management and discovered she was not covering for her morning carbohydrates sufficiently and was complaining of headaches in the morning. The nurse set up the related school nursing service of meeting with her daily to review her morning diet and medications. After a series of one-on-one meetings with the student and in collaboration with her physician, the student was better able to self-manage her diabetes and keep her academic progress on track.

Key Factors in IDEA 2004 Revised Law
Response to Intervention (RtI)

One key factor of IDEA 2004 is that it offers two approaches for determining a student's eligibility for services related to learning disabilities. Prior to 2004, the approach was to monitor and evaluate the child for a severe discrepancy between achievement and intellectual abilities. A new process in IDEA 2004, the response to intervention (RtI), can determine if the response of a child with a disability to the latest research-based intervention—the preventive, remedial, or compensatory services given the child and used as a benchmark—identifies a student's need for special education. RtI is a framework for implementing proactive, data-driven decision-making that provides educators better and more-timely information about students to improve their learning and performance. Many students can function successfully in the classroom with just a little bit of additional support.

If RtI is successful, there is no need to move to a full case study evaluation (CSE). If, however, after several RtI trials the student is not responding in a positive way, the special education team should complete a detailed (CSE) after obtaining the parents' or guardians' written permission.

The school nurse should work with the classroom teacher to implement RtI support if needed. If involved early, the school nurse will have a better understanding of whether a student may move forward to a complete CSE. RtI support will be covered more in depth in chapter 3.

Functional Behavior Analysis

Another key factor in IDEA 2004 is a functional behavior analysis (also known as a functional behavior assessment). The analysis or assessment leads to a plan to improve a student's negative behavior in the classroom. This plan is offered by the classroom teacher and the special education team. Through the IDEA, the role of the parents is strengthened as they are asked to participate in this analysis by discussing their child's strengths and concerns and documenting them on the IEP form.

Parents are also involved in the process of manifestation determination, which is used to course action related to behavioral concerns. Before any special education student can be subject to suspension due to serious behavior issues, the FBA and IEP are considered alongside the manifestation determination meeting involving the parents and special education team that must take place within ten school days of any decision to change the placement of a child with a disability because of a violation of school code.

The IEP team, which includes several stakeholders (and is covered in depth in chapter 3), must review all relevant information in the student's file to determine if the conduct in question was caused by the child's disability or was a direct result of the school district's failure to implement the child's IEP.

Other Education Laws and Legal Precedents Related to School Nursing and the Courts

Two United States Supreme Court cases are considered foundational in establishing the requirement that students with special health care needs must have their health care needs met at school by school personnel if the health care is needed for the student to receive a free appropriate public education (FAPE) and the health care can be provided by a nonphysician. In some jurisdictions, these cases are referred to as the cases establishing the requirement that students with special health care needs receive required nursing services and that nurses are a related support service provider.

On July 5, 1984, in *Irving Independent School District v. Tatro*, the US Supreme Court decided on the case presented to them by the Irving, Texas, school district claiming that neither the Education of the Handicapped Act nor the Rehabilitation Act of 1973 required a school district to provide a handicapped child with clean intermittent catheterization (CIC) during school hours. The school district held that CIC was a medical service and that medical services were specifically excluded from those laws as required to be provided. Lower courts had ruled first against and then on appeal in favor of the parents' request. The school district appealed. The Supreme Court ruled that a medical service was one that could be performed only by a physician for purposes of diagnosis or evaluation and that since CIC could be performed by nonphysicians, it was therefore a related service to be provided under those laws. By extension, similar health services that could be performed by other than medical doctors began to be accepted as required related services.

On November 4, 1998, in *Cedar Rapids Community School District v. Garret F.*, the US Supreme Court heard the case presented to them by the Cedar Rapids, Iowa, school district claiming it did not need to provide the complicated nursing services required for a student to attend the school. Given the court's decision in *Tatro*, the school board did not argue that Garret's care constituted medical services. Instead, it proposed that several other factors should be considered including "whether the care is continuous or intermittent" and the expense of the services.

On March 3, 1999, the Court ruled 7–2 in favor of the student that the 1990 IDEA required school boards to provide continuous nursing services to disabled students who need them during the school day.

Under the IDEA and the court's own precedent, the justices ruled that a school board must fund such related services to help guarantee that students such as Garret were integrated into the public schools.

The *Cedar Rapids v. Garret* case set the standard that schools must provide nursing services no matter the cost or complexity if the care needed could be performed by a nurse rather than solely by a physician or similar health care provider and at no cost to the parents.

School nurses must have a deep understanding of this and similar IDEA laws and court cases. In their daily practice in school, nurses must also ensure that students' confidentiality and privacy are maintained in accordance with the following laws: Family Educational Rights and Privacy Act (FERPA, 1974), 20 U.S.C. § 1232g; 34 CFR Part 99, and the Health Information Portability and Accountability Act. The text of these cases and documents can be found online and through school nurse resources.

FERPA

FERPA (Family Educational Rights and Privacy Act), enacted in 1974, applies to all schools and districts receiving federal funds; it is a law that protects the privacy of student education records. The law refers to student health records as also being part of the education record, so all parts of FERPA apply equally to academic and health records and any other written documentation about the student. All records created or maintained by the school nurse are considered part of the educational record. Following FERPA provisions prevents unauthorized disclosure of these records.

FERPA requires that schools must have a written records release from a parent or guardian but allows several exceptions. FERPA allows schools to disclose records without consent to school officials who have legitimate educational interests in them and to other schools to which a student transfers. Parents, guardians, or eligible students can review the students' records and ask for amendments to the records with written request to the school. Schools may also disclose directory information but must allow the parent or guardian an opportunity to not permit disclosure of directory information. In addition, US code 20 U.S.C. § 1232g; 34 CFR Part 99 specifies that the school must notify parents of their FERPA rights via a letter, bulletin, handbook, and so forth.

HIPAA

On the other hand, the 1996 Health Information Portability and Accountability Act (HIPAA) is not an education law but a health and human services law. This law applies to health plans, health care providers (HCPs), and health care clearinghouses for data. School nurses are of course health care providers in the common use of the term, but in their work in educational settings, they are not normally subject to HIPAA but are always subject to FERPA privacy rules. School nurses may in some narrow circumstances such as school-based clinics that are part of a clinical entity also be subject to HIPAA rules.

As FERPA supersedes HIPAA in school settings, all school staff and especially school nurses must be knowledgeable and aware of FERPA restrictions regarding disclosure of a student's information in and outside the school setting. School nurses may have or may still be working in health care institutions and have a good understanding of HIPAA regulations applicable to those settings, but they must be able to differentiate between and be able to apply both laws. The laws allow for individual health and medical information to be protected while still allowing for the exchange of needed information to provide students with services by permitting information disclosures to others as needed and within the terms of the respective laws.

With either law, dissemination of information needed to provide the best nursing care possible in the school setting is allowable with written parental permission. With the protection of both laws, students' private information is protected while allowing for others to obtain the critical information needed to provide the best nursing care possible in school.

Other Privacy Considerations

School districts should keep all student records secure in locked filing cabinets. Since FERPA defines a student's educational record as anything in his or her file, this assurance of secured/locked records should be effective for all student records whether academic or medical. In addition, the school must make sure if using electronic records that they are accessible only via a password-protected health information system.

In collaboration with the administration and staff, the role of district nurse regarding student confidentiality is to properly educate staff and ensure that students' rights to confidentiality and privacy are maintained and that applicable FERPA and HIPAA laws are followed.

Section 504 Plan

Section 504 is the section of the Vocational Rehabilitation Act of 1973 that prohibits discrimination against all individuals with disabilities in programs that receive federal funds. The concept was further clarified in the Americans with Disabilities Act Amendment Act (ADAAA) of 2008, which amended the civil rights law passed in 1990 that protects individuals with disabilities from discrimination and requires building and transportation accessibility and reasonable accommodations in the workplace, including a more inclusive and broad range of disabilities.

To qualify for a Section 504 plan, "a student must be determined to: (1) have a physical or mental impairment that substantially limits one or more major life activities; or (2) have a record of such an impairment; or (3) be regarded as having such an impairment" (US Department of Education 2010).

Disability refers to a physical or mental impairment that substantially limits a major life activity. Except for ordinary eyeglasses and contact lenses, schools cannot consider the effect of mitigating measures such as medication, in determining whether someone has a disability. Impairments that are episodic or in remission can be considered disabilities if they substantially limit a major life activity when active.

Under the amended ADA law, the list of potentially impacted major life activities was expanded to include caring for oneself, performing manual tasks, seeing, hearing, eating, sleeping, walking, standing, lifting, bending, speaking, breathing, learning, reading, concentrating, thinking, communicating, and working (US Congress 2008). With this amendment, more students are qualifying for Section 504 plans. The school must make appropriate, also known as "reasonable,"[4] accommodations for student with disabilities.

In one school, this might be a student with asthma having trouble keeping up in gym and class activities. Required modifications or accommodations for that student might include the following:

- an adaptive PE plan
- an air-conditioned classroom
- teaching and assistance with medication administration
- recommending a support group for the student
- teaching signs of crisis
- providing an emergency action plan (EAP), which is usually written by the school nurse to assist all school staff to provide care to a child with a known, life-threatening health condition

In another school, the modification may mean a child with sickle cell disease has his physical education class earlier in the day before he is physically tired and perhaps in mild to moderate pain. It may mean a student with diabetes has his or her most difficult class immediately after lunch or snack, when the brain has fuel and is better suited to thinking and problem solving. For some students, a physical education teacher licensed or trained in designing adapted physical education (APE) programs will need to create a specially designed physical education program using accommodations physical and/or cognitive designed to fit the needs of students who require developmental or corrective instruction.

While IDEA requires students to show progress, Section 504 does not require the student to show progress but only access to the general education program. However, access may be all some students need to succeed. A student with an orthopedic impairment may need only access to the classroom to succeed in a course that is provided on an upper floor. A student without that disability may access his education by climbing stairs. Building or installing a ramp may be all that is needed, and a Section 504 plan may guarantee that the student has the key to the elevator or other accommodation so he can make it to class on time. A Section 504 accommodation plan

---

[4] Since the term *reasonable* is often defined differently among the parties involved, there is movement away from the term *reasonable* toward *appropriate and necessary* accommodations. The term *reasonable* is sometimes used incorrectly to refer to the related aids and services in the elementary and secondary school context (US Department of Education 2015).

ensures that students with disabilities have an equal opportunity to participate in school programs and extracurricular activities.

Accommodations and Modifications of Environment

Accommodations and modifications of environment describes the services and the program modification to be provided to the student. Classroom accommodations can be made across educational settings such as the general education classroom, the resource room, or special classes. Changes can be made to seating arrangements, lighting, sound, food and drink privileges, bathroom privileges, use of staff or equipment elevator if not normally permitted for students to use, and other rules or practices that may need to be modified for this student to have access to his or her education. The school nurse may write those necessary accommodations to support the student on the IEP or Section 504 form whether handwritten, typed, or in electronic form. Some examples of common modifications and accommodations are in appendix 2.

For example, a student with a hearing deficit may be seated closer to the front of the class or where the majority of the teaching will occur. That student may be allowed to move to other locations in the class or lab to better see the instruction as well as hear it, while a student without the disability may be required to stay seated. A student who uses a wheelchair may be provided a safe ramp at an access point different from those used by other students including a bus loading and unloading area.

Modifications to the curriculum generally require special education services, and plans to significantly alter the scope or content of the general education curriculum though Section 504 plans can include minor measures such as reducing the number but not the difficulty of test questions or administering a test in a room with no distractions.

SECTION 2

The Special Education Process

CHAPTER 3

From Referral to Case Study

The special education process involves a number of sequential procedures or steps. The first step is a written referral concerning the student's learning issues. Students generally enter the special education referral process in one of two ways:

1. A parent, teacher, member of the school personnel, state agency, community service agency, and/or health care provider notices a potential problem a child in school or of preschool age has and makes a referral. The type of referral depends on the school district as every school district has a different method to start this referral process. In some for example, a parent may fill out referral forms or send a personal letter or email to the school principal.

   If the district believes the referral is appropriate, the school will hold an assessment planning meeting hereinafter referred to as the domain meeting to discuss the child's learning or behavior issues at school.

2. The student did not do well with response to intervention (RtI) interventions, which may be initially conducted when a student is having difficulty with learning and is not achieving to the expected level. RtI meetings determine what interventions or assistance may be offered that may benefit the student. Those interventions offer a tier of options within the multi-tier system of supports, a framework that many schools use to target support to struggling students. This RtI meeting should include an invitation for the school nurse, who will need to come prepared with information about all educational interventions available for a student with a medical diagnosis if any. If the student is still not successful after this meeting and the implementation of the RtI process stemming from it, the school will go to the next step, the domain meeting.

The Domain Meeting

The second step in the process is a domain meeting. A domain is one of eight areas of potential concern that federal law requires schools to discuss as part of the student's evaluation for special education services (see below). At this meeting, the school or district's special education team and parents discuss initial findings or opinions about the student's domains and determine which domains need more attention and require full evaluations prior to determining eligibility for special education.

A full evaluation may be required in all domains by district policy or when the meeting participants determine that not enough is known about the child in specific domains and that more testing is required in one or more of the areas, what tests will be administered, and who will gather the information.

A critical component of the professional school nurse's toolbox is keen observation of the student. Based on that and other information, the school nurse may suggest more medical and educational testing that could lead to some students' previously unknown or undiscovered health issues being evaluated fully. It is very important for the nurse to have a framework of information to provide participants in the domain meeting and be prepared to discuss how much more evaluation is prudent in the health, vision, or hearing domain to rule out any medical issues that may be affecting the student's learning in school.[5]

This domain meeting will be held at the initial evaluation and repeated periodically (at least every three years) as the student progresses if his or her academic progress or lack of it warrants continuing with and meeting eligibility for special education services.

The eight domain areas are these:

- academic achievement
- functional performance
- cognitive functioning
- communication
- health
- vision and hearing
- motor ability
- social-emotional status

It is best practice, and for some students it is vital, for the school nurse to attend the domain meeting with the other IEP team members and include the parents to discuss the medical, health, vision, and hearing results.

Other information about the child may rule out initial suspicions of a medical issue or lead

---

[5] The terms *impact*, *affect*, and *adverse effect* on learning are often used interchangeably by members of IEP teams to mean essentially the same thing: a specific condition of the disability that prevents a student from achievement at least partially due to that condition. The authors also use the terms interchangeably to condition the reader to those terms as currently used among special education practitioners.

to the need for more information or examination by a physician or primary care practitioner to possibly diagnose medical issues that might interfere with the child's learning.

At this meeting, the nurse can request a release from the parents for more information or past medical records. In most states, vision and hearing are assessed yearly including whether the student has been prescribed corrective vision aids and if so whether they are being utilized appropriately.

In the three-year evaluation of a student, if the domain area of health has been addressed more than three years prior (ideally more recently), team members will encourage the student to be screened for any new or existing medical issues that could affect his or her learning.

After each domain is discussed with the parents, the IEP team and parents may conclude there is evidence to move forward with a full evaluation for special education (known as a case study), and most often, the parents sign written consent. To consent, the parent must have been fully informed in his or her preferred language or other mode of communication of all the information about the action for which he or she is providing consent, and the parent then affirms that he or she understands and agrees in writing to that action.

IDEA 2004 requires that more than one instrument of evaluation is to be used for each domain being evaluated. For example, one IQ test alone cannot determine cognitive function, one developmental questionnaire alone cannot determine social/developmental status, and one parent interview alone cannot determine the state of the student's health. In some school districts, the classroom teacher or case manager will assess the student's learning environment and discuss the findings in the IEP meeting.

The parent is not required to agree to any or all of the evaluation components, but if the corresponding clinician who would be conducting that component believes strongly in the need for the evaluation, he or she may want to meet with the parent to discuss the value of the information that may be obtained. Some parents may decline due to fear of lack of privacy; the nurse will want to reiterate the pledge that nurses make to protect confidentiality and explain what may or may not be shared within the school and how any information shared outside the school would need the parents' written permission to release.

If the parents do not agree to a portion of the evaluation, the clinician (nurse if the portion is health evaluation) should document in writing the parents' lack of consent to whatever manner or format is indicated by the school or district. The district may conclude that further evaluation is not needed to provide instruction for the student. If the district determines not to conduct an evaluation, it shall provide written notice of that to the parents.

Moving Forward to Case Study

To summarize the process to this point, the school nurse and the team have completed the first step, considering a referral, and the second step, participating in a domain meeting. At the domain meeting, if the parties agreed that a case study evaluation (CSE) is indicated, written consent was obtained.

The third step is to complete further evaluation, also called a case study. Further evaluation is required before a student may be found eligible for an IEP.[6] The school nurse should be aware that the evaluations in the health domain as well as all others must be completed within the required sixty school days of parental written consent. Most school special education administrators will list that due date on the notice to staff who are to complete the evaluations, and the school nurse must be aware of that due date.

Flow Chart for Development of a Student's IEP

Initial Eligibility:

- Historical data
- Standardized assessments
- Diagnostic assessment
- Curriculum-based assessment (CBA)
- Parents' and student's input
- Medical reports, health history, current health status, nurse physical assessment of student

IEP Development:

- Identify one or more of the thirteen disabilities
- Develop Present Level of Academic Achievement and Functional Performance (PLAAFP)
- Develop goals, benchmarks, and short-term objectives
- Determine least restrictive environment (LRE) and special education and related services needed to support the student

IEP Implementation:

- Assign appropriate staff
- Monitor student's progress
- Collect progress data
- Document services

Continuous Progress Monitoring:

- Analyze data to evaluate effectiveness of instruction and related services from school nurses to the student
- Adjust instruction or related service as necessary
- Review/revise IEP at least annually (or earlier, if there are concerns about making progress toward achieving the goal)

[6] School districts may have different names for this meeting including multidisciplinary staffing meeting or full individual evaluation meeting.

Members of the IEP Team

Federal law—IDEA 2004, Section 1414(d)(1)(B)—requires that the school's IEP team consists of at minimum these participants:

- the parents[7] of a child with a disability
- at least one general education teacher of the child if he or she is or may be participating in the regular education environment
- at least one special education teacher or where appropriate at least one special education provider of such child
- a representative of the local educational agency[8]
- someone who can interpret the instructional implications of evaluation results
- at the discretion of the parent or the agency, other individuals who have knowledge of or special expertise regarding the child including related services personnel as appropriate and whenever appropriate the child with the disability
- other person(s) having knowledge of the child such as the child's private therapist may also attend with parental consent
- at the parents' request, a legal representative or parental advocate (an individual such as an independent consultant or representative of an organization dedicated to persons with disabilities) who works to ensure that parents understand their rights and that school professionals provide an appropriate education
- the child with disabilities may also attend

The federal requirement of an "individual who can interpret the instructional implications of evaluation results" and "other individuals who have knowledge or special expertise … including related services personnel" supports the inclusion of the school nurse in the IEP team as well as other qualified professionals including the school psychologist, the school social worker, the school counselor, and the child's case manager if there is one. It is very important that the child's school has

---

[7] In this book, the term *parent* will be used to include all other definitions or understandings of who may be a parent as described in 34 C.F.R. 300.20: a parent is defined as a natural or adoptive parent of a child, a guardian (but not the state if the child is a ward of the state), a person acting in the place of a parent (such as a grandparent or stepparent with whom the child lives, or a person who is legally responsible for the child's welfare), or a surrogate parent. (US Department of Education, April 16 2001) https://sites.ed.gov/idea/idea-files/policy-letter-april-16-2001-to-pinal-county-arizona-deputy-county-attorney-linda-l-harant/. Accessed March 30, 2019.

[8] A representative of the local educational agency is often an administrator, one identified by the district as the professional responsible for managing some aspect of schools; most often a principal, assistant principal, or special education chief but may also include department chairs, team leaders, special coordinators, district administrators, and others.

a great partnership with the parents founded on open and honest communication and collaboration among all team members including parent and student when possible.

The qualifications of the personnel who will evaluate and if needed provide services are established by each state education agency (SEA) under federal law; see "Establishes the responsibility of the SEA for personnel qualifications" in 34 CFR 300.156(a).[9] The qualifications must be consistent with any state-approved or state-recognized certification, licensing, registration, or other comparable requirements that apply to the professional discipline in which those personnel are providing special education or related services. In some states, the RN must possess additional credentials or certifications. The required credentials may vary by state, and in some states, a medical doctor, district physician, or other medical personnel are deemed qualified to perform the health/medical evaluation.

The Body of the Full Evaluation (Case Study)

The major portion of the special education process is the full case study, which will result in the student being determined eligible or not for special education services.

To reiterate, a student must have one of the thirteen disabilities identified under IDEA 2004 listed in appendix 1 to be eligible for special education and related services.

The Role of the School Nurse in the Case Study

The school nurse takes an active role on the IEP team. The school nurse will conduct a complete health history or medical review (the terms being interchangeable or different among states). If the school nurse indicates any health, vision, or hearing concerns, she or he will follow up with a complete assessment of the child to determine eligibility for special education and related services for the child with the IEP team at the IEP meeting.

For a child's initial case study, a thorough health history/medical review is important because this may be the first time health and education interactions are considered. Additionally, as nurses rarely perform health assessments or nursing assessments without observing the patient, the school nurse needs to have observed the child to perform a complete evaluation. Such evaluation, observation, and study help the team make the best educational placement decisions and plans for any related services for the child in the school setting.

[9] A link to the Code of Federal Regulations related to special education is in appendix 3.

The Nursing Process and Its Application in the Special Education Evaluation

Nurses in any practice setting use the nursing process as a systematic approach to complete their work regardless of whether the setting is the Intensive Care Unit, the school, or the nursing home. The process is integral to identifying the client's needs, creating a plan, and evaluating the necessary nursing interventions.

Similarly, the nursing process in the special education setting is parallel to the nursing process in other practice settings. In school, it begins with gathering medical information in a systematic manner so that it plays a role in making a legal and instructional decision that a student needs or does not need special education services. The nursing process contributes to a better understanding of the student's physical and health strengths, weaknesses, and limitations in determining what supports or services the student needs to succeed in school.

The work of evaluation should follow a structured procedure following the six elements of the nursing process: assessment, diagnosis, outcome identification, planning, implementation, and evaluation of the plan. The nursing process is described in many nursing textbooks. The procedure is also sometimes referred to by the acronym SOAP or SOAPIE (subjective, objective, assessment, plan, implementation, and evaluation). These steps may provide guidance for nurses unfamiliar with the nursing process in special education evaluation procedures.

Step 1—Assessment

The IEP data collection phase helps determine the student's current health status and any actual or potential health concerns.

Step 2—Diagnosis

The school nurse uses the assessment data to formulate a nursing diagnosis including a diagnostic label, etiology, and presenting signs and symptoms in the educational setting.

Step 3—Outcome Identification

The nurse identifies the desired results of nursing intervention and states these in measurable terms.

Step 4—Planning

Interventions are selected to achieve desired results for a student's IEP goal.

Step 5—Implementation

The student's written IEP is put in practice, and care provided is documented.

Step 6—Evaluation

The nurse measures the effectiveness of the student's IEP in meeting the identified outcome. Changes are made to the program as need.

The nursing assessment has come to be commonly known as the medical review in some states, but other states may call it something else. Each state, school, or nurse may follow a different form or format to complete the health evaluation. For example, each state sets its own criteria for what determines appropriate hearing and vison screening. Federal law does not offer a specific title to this nursing evaluation other than vision, hearing, or health, but regardless of the title or name of the evaluation, it is a complete health evaluation of the student including nursing and medical aspects.

Federal law requires that a student who is being evaluated or reevaluated for special education services must be provided an assessment "in all areas related to the suspected disability, including, if appropriate, health, vision, [and] hearing" (US Department of Education, 34 CFR 300.304, Evaluation Procedures).

Regardless of the formal name or structure of the health evaluation process, the steps of each parallel components of a well-written and likely legally defensible IEP health evaluation documentation.

To summarize, in the context of the case study, the school nurse has the following responsibilities:

- to conduct a full study of the student's health (defined in IDEA as a health evaluation but also known in some states as medical review, health assessment, health review, or similar terminology)
- to obtain data that may be conducted or found in the school system as well as external sources
- to complete a written assessment report including the medical/health summary indicating any medical/health conditions present that may have an adverse effect on the student's learning
- to interpret and analyze at the team meeting the medical/health data collected by the nurse and others directed by the nurse
- to discuss the student's educational needs
- to recommend the appropriate educational program and any needed related services based on the student's health needs

CHAPTER 4

Assessment of a Student's Health

Identification of Evaluation Components to Be Conducted

All state education departments have rules or instructions dealing with student educational evaluations for special education purposes. Before beginning the time-consuming task of conducting an assessment and creating educational goals, the nurse should check her state's education agency rules or requirements for the assessment. Though the language may seem very formal, it is important to keep in mind that this process is not new to nurses as RNs have always completed a detailed medical health history upon the admission or check-in of a patient in different settings such as hospitals, clinical settings, or home care.

The purpose of the school nurse assessment is to review the current medical examination (ideally one performed within the previous school year) and a vision and hearing screening (also within the previous school year or more recently). It is vital for the school nurse to understand a student's past and current medical examination and any other medical information for the purpose of the nursing assessment and planning for the student who is being referred.

The school nurse may perform a physical assessment to complement the most recent medical examinations. Part of the formal examination may include detailed medical history, an examination of the functioning of cranial nerves, the student's vision, hearing, and balance, and if indicated particularly in a younger child, a neurological screening performed by a physician or nurse. The neurological screening may be provided on the student's physical examination or other medical reports. The physician may request other special medical procedures and other important tests if the physician has concerns about the child's medical condition.

In regard to special education, the most universal role of the school nurse in the nursing assessment process is as the coordinator of health data in terms of requesting, collecting, and reviewing all the necessary medical records before the formal IEP meeting. School nurses work with physicians, clinical psychologists, school psychologists, school counselors, school social workers, speech-language specialists, occupational therapists (OTs), physical therapists (PTs), and others to serve as members of the multidisciplinary educational teams. They collaborate with educational colleagues, parents, and community health professionals to promote the health and learning of students and eliminate barriers to academic success.

This evaluation of health is not an isolated nursing activity but a process with several activities resulting in a complete review of the student's medical and health status. It will provide the answer to the question, is a health condition adversely affecting a student's educational performance, and if so, how should it be addressed to help the student improve academically?

The number of activities is determined by the nurse, who has responsibility for the evaluation. The activities usually include these elements:

- screening or exam results of vision and hearing and a review of body systems
- interviews with the parent, student, teacher, teacher assistant, and others as appropriate
- a review of the sick or injury visits to the nurse or health office including any noted patterns
- accident, incident, or disciplinary reports
- results of the most recent physical examination and any other documents or interviews that each part of the review would indicate leads to further investigation (e.g., an EEG report from a hospital following a concussion or follow-up for seizures, lab reports for lead screening, etc.)

The nurse will utilize the science and art of nursing and trust the education, training, and keen senses to lead the nurse to investigate behavior or symptoms that seem out of kilter.

Just as a nurse's notes on a hospital admission follow a certain protocol, methods, or instruments for some of the assessments (e.g., coma scales, admission blood tests, ECG for chest pain, etc.), the school nurse has similar protocols and instruments. Each state sets its own criteria for what determines an appropriate hearing and vision screening, for example.

Before a nurse begins such screenings, she or he must learn what is required or allowed such as state certification in those screenings, whether an eye chart is sufficient, and if a muscle balance test is required. Screening for color deficiency might be required. Hearing tests might have to be conducted at certain decibel levels (a measure of loudness) and frequencies (a measure of pitch) as well as air conduction vs. bone conduction.

When the nurse must pull the student out of class for any component of the assessment, the time out of class should be as little as possible and ideally not at the time of the student's favorite activities or classes in which the student is struggling.

Other questions to be answered are these:

- Can some of the components be done before or after the school day?
- Can the student eat lunch with the nurse while some of the evaluation or screenings are done?

- Can the hearing or vision screening be incorporated into the routine school-wide screening to not cause undue focus, teasing, or stigmatization from peers?
- Can the general observation be done while the student is with peers on the playground or at physical education or recess?
- If the student will be pulled out for an interview, can a joint interview with the social worker be conducted to minimize minutes away from the classroom?

A joint interview may also help each clinician learn more about what the other professional attempts to draw out of the student have revealed, and that may lead to follow-up questions posed by the partnering clinicians. In some districts, a written questionnaire is provided in advance to the parent, but it should always be followed up with a personal interview.

For example, observing the awkward physical activity of a male toddler during the parent interview at home, which the parent shrugged off as "It's just how he is," may trigger the nurse to encourage the parent to have the child further examined for any physical anomalies. In one case, these questions and suggestions led the student to be examined and later diagnosed with muscular dystrophy.

Similarly, a student whose outbursts in class and at home were labeled as a behavior disorder led the nurse to create a referral to pediatric neurology, which resulted in the diagnosis of a seizure disorder. With appropriate seizure medication, the child's seemingly irrational behavior diminished, and she was able to grow academically and socially.

Consider for example a five-year-old kindergartener who was unable to copy a circle or hold a pencil correctly. The school nurse may discuss this concern with the parents and occupational therapist (OT), and with parental consent, the occupational therapist at school may observe the student to rule out any fine motor concerns. The school nurse and/or occupational therapist may each seek written parental consent or a release of information to be signed so both nurse and OT can ask the health care provider for a written order for further evaluation by an OT. (Check state laws regarding practice regulations for OT, as some states may allow independent practice without referral from an MD.)

After collecting all the medical records for the student, the school nurse uses critical skill techniques and nursing deductions to determine if any other important medical reports or additional screening is needed to complete the school nurse report for the IEP.

The school nurse is concerned about any medical issues of the child; the nurse must bring it to the attention of the parents and discuss a plan for addressing it. The school nurse cannot require the parents to take the student for further testing but may suggest that they bring up these issues at the next scheduled medical visit. The nurse should know if a required school physical examination is coming up soon and could suggest that it be conducted during the allowable sixty-day period if the exam would also meet the timeframe allowable for entry into the school or next grade level.

The nurse may provide the parents with a written nursing referral for them to give to the health care provider. If provided, a copy of this written referral should be kept in the student's health folder and a notation in the student's special education files as well.

The school nurse needs to follow the school's request for the release of information procedure when requesting or releasing medical information to and from the school. If the child has any chronic health condition such as attention deficit hyperactivity disorder (ADHD), seizures, asthma, and so on, the school and parents should sign a release of information form before the IEP meeting. Such a release may be useful for both IEP and general student health issues that may occur.

During the nursing assessment process, the nurse may discover that the student may need other formal testing by the school psychologist or social worker. The nurse should share such concerns with the other team members. Sometimes, the team will discuss or seek certain testing for the student.

Health History Interview

The health history includes objective and subjective data; some information in it may be measurable and in official records (birth certificates, hospitalization notes, etc.) while other information is subjective (parental or student recall of health and physical development). It is not the only component of the school nurse evaluation, but it is very critical. This informal interview is key to understanding the child's prenatal and postnatal history, early health issues, child development, and high-risk behaviors, and that is worth additional mention here.

It is very important to solicit key information from the parent or guardian to understand the early or current health issues of the student.

Although foster parents may not know all of a child's health history, parents or guardians who have been part of their child's life since birth should know answers to these questions, which should include these:

- Was this a high-risk pregnancy? If so, in what way?
- Age of mother at child's birth?
- Was there prenatal care?
- When was the first visit to a physician or nurse?
- Birth weight? Full term? Premature?
- Did the baby go home with the mother at her discharge?
- Did the child have any sucking problems or problems with breastfeeding or bottle-feeding?
- Did the child have a hearing test before being discharged? Results?
- Did the child receive early intervention services (EIS)? Why?
- Is there any individualized family service plan (IFSP) you can share with me?

- Did your child have any serious illness or hospitalization during the first year of life?
- Did you have any concerns about your child's developmental milestones?
- Frequent ear infections? How many?
- Do you understand your child's speech? Do other family members understand your child's speech?
- Any history of lead poisoning or exposure to lead paint, water, and the like?
- Any medication given in the past? Currently on medication? If in the past but not now, did you stop giving the medications on your own, or did the health care provider discontinue them?
- Based on available documentation, what is the student's medical diagnosis?
- Medical records? Dates? Any more recent? Pending medical visits?
- What is the purpose of each medication and its potential benefit?
- Does the medication cause side effects or adverse reactions?
- What are the effects of the medication on the student's educational performance?
- What is your view of medication?
- Has the child had a full eye examination? Do you notice if your child's eyes cross or wander? Any concern? Surgery?
- Can your child dress himself/herself? Fully or some?
- Is your child toilet trained? If yes, when did that occur? Any accidents?
- Is your child sad, angry, or very active?

Other Questions for Student if Developmentally Appropriate

- Any health issues such as asthma or any allergies to food, insects, chemicals, and so forth?
- Any medical issues? Recent ER visits? Hospitalizations?
- Taking medication in school or out of school? Prescription or OTC drugs? At what times?
- Taking any vitamins at home? Supplements?
- Student's view of medication?

Vision Issues

- Does the student have a vision or eye condition? Past surgery? Improvement?
- What is the student's near and distant best corrected acuity?
- Last vision acuity? Date of screening? Past history?
- Need vision function examination?
- Does the student have a color vision impairment?

- Past eye examination? If screened, pass or fail? Unable to test?
- Broken glasses?
- Last time wearing glasses? Wears them in school?

Hearing Issues

- Does the student have any hearing loss? Its nature and degree?
- If appropriate, describe the speech awareness thresholds and/or speech reception thresholds.
- Does the student have personal amplification? If so, describe. Examples include cochlear implants or hearing aids.
- Is the student a consistent wearer of his or her personal amplification system?
- Last time wearing it in school? In the classroom?
- Does the student report dysfunction of his or her personal amplification system when appropriate?
- How does the student's hearing loss impact auditory functioning in school?
- Lip reading? Where does student sit in classroom? By teacher in front or back?
- Speech patterns?

Motor Issues

- Does the student have motor issues that affect educational performance including the ability to sit, stand, and move in the classroom and in the school in general?
- Does the student have any difficulty transferring to and from a wheelchair, desk chair, toilet, and so on?
- Does the student have sensory motor challenges? If so, describe.
- Does the student have fine motor deficits? If so, describe.
- Needs an elevator? Ramp? Any bus concerns?
- Transportation with wheelchair?

Other Questions to Consider Asking for the Assessment Process

- Does the student's medical condition result in limited strength, vitality, or alertness that limits productivity?
- Does the student require assistance with activities of daily living (ADL) such as dressing, toileting, feeding?
- Does the student's medical condition restrict activity at school?

- Do mobility issues require safety precautions, for instance at the bus, playground, or gym?
- How does the student currently use assistive technology (AT), computer-driven or electronic tools, equipment, and applications designed to help him or her with disabilities, to learn, to communicate, and otherwise to function more independently by bypassing the disabilities or other special equipment?
- Mood, affect, speech pattern, voice?
- Nonverbal student?
- Is the student medically fragile? What is the status of Do Not Resuscitate (DNR) orders if any? Have such orders for palliative care been considered? Does the student need care provided by a one-on-one nurse or paraprofessional?

Parents' Concerns

During the assessment procedures, it is very important to ask the parents or guardians their educational and medical concerns for the student. Other family members involved with the child such as grandparents, babysitters, or after-school care providers if relevant and with parental permission may provide additional information and may offer different or corroborating perceptions of the child's performance in school and at home. If permitted, ask the person who picks the child up if he or she has noticed any issues with the child's health or education; seek email addresses of the child's other family members and particularly older or adult siblings who may have known the child for years and have their own suggestions or observations.

It is very important to ask the parents about their child's strengths too. Parents should be active participants in the decisions concerning their child's education, but all too often, they come to an IEP evaluation meeting anxiously thinking they will hear nothing but their child's deficits, struggles, and failures. The nurse as well as all other staff involved in the evaluation should find positive attributes of the student for the sake of the parents. For example, does the student come to school well groomed? Is the child physically active and enjoy recess? Does the student say he enjoys a well-rounded source of nutrition? Is the student polite and friendly to staff and fellow classmates? Does the student exhibit a great sense of humor? Any information that can lead the parents to smile about their child is helpful and encouraging especially in the stressful setting of an IEP team meeting.

Teachers' Concerns

For the school nurse assessment procedures, it is very important that the nurse ask the student's classroom teachers about their concerns or observations of the student's educational achievements and behavior. As the people at school who see the student daily and probably more than any other student partner except his or her parents, they can share their concerns about the child with the nurse. They of course will also likely be in attendance at the student meeting later in the process, but this is an opportunity for the nurse to learn their take on the child's specific health and mental health issues. It is very important that school nurses develop good working relationships with the school staff to understand the student's unique needs or concerns.

Student Interviews

A visit with the student, including an interview when possible, is a required component of most IEP evaluation procedures. Preschoolers who are being evaluated should also be interviewed, taking into account their developmental stages. The student interview regardless of the student's age or cognitive abilities should always be respectful and should be included in the data gathered for the case study.

Most nurses can deftly interview a student as part of an IEP evaluation. Nurses with significant pediatric experience have learned how to have age-appropriate conversations with particularly young patients. The interview questions will need to be adapted for developmental age and existing health conditions. However, when a nurse is talking with a student being evaluated for special education, the conversation may also need to be revised to adapt to the cognitive or developmental issues specific to the student.

The nurse should find a space for the interview that is quiet but also visible to other adults and then explain to the student the purpose of the interview—to learn more about him or her so the nurse can better serve the student. If the student provides more information about the purpose such as, "It's because I'm stupid, right?" or failing, or other language indicating poor self-esteem, the nurse can assure the student that he or she has positive qualities and that the nurse wants to learn more about those things and what the student thinks about them. That will allow the nurse to begin the interview with questions or observations that will strengthen the student's positive aspects. Prior discussion by the nurse with the parent and teachers will inform the nurse who may not know this student particularly well about the student's strengths and positive aspects.

Throughout the meeting with the student, the nurse can observe the student's manner, appearance, and eye contact or lack of that. The following list offers some suggestions for interview questions and discussion items, but by all means, the nurse should listen to the student and pick up on issues that concern him or her. The nurse should allow the student to lead the discussion even if it meanders rather than follow a formal checklist that the student might view as a test of sorts, which might prompt the student to shut down or provide answers he or she thinks the nurse is casting about for.

The school nurse may select from this list any questions that may be appropriate for the age or abilities of the student or ask others based on his or her prior experiences with children of any age:

- What time to you go to bed? Do you text or listen to TV before bed? If yes, how many hours?
- Any sleep problems? Phobias? Nightmares?
- What time do you wake up on school days?
- Do you eat breakfast? What do you eat? Lunch at school?
- Any friends in school?
- What school activities do you participate in? Clubs or sports in or outside school?
- When was the last time you saw a doctor or health care provider? For what?
- What are you concerned about in school?
- What problems do you have in school? With what subjects?
- Are you passing your subjects?
- What subjects do you need help with?
- How often and how much do you access, view, or participate in social media? Do you have any concerns about what is written about you or any photos others may have posted online that embarrass you?
- Do you have any questions for me?

The questions the nurse asks parents may also be asked of the student if they are developmentally appropriate. In some cases, the concerns of the parents may be drastically different from the student's concerns.

Observation of the Student

The student's classroom observation can be handled by any number and combination of team members: nurse, classroom teacher, social worker, and school psychologist as per school policy. Each team member will provide observation data relevant to his or her area of expertise.

The school nurse will observe the child in the classroom or for a preschooler in a natural setting such as home, childcare setting, or playground to perform a well-rounded nursing assessment. It is particularly important that the nurse observe the child if the nurse is considering providing nursing interventions to the student within the IEP or even if another nurse is currently providing the services. This observation gives the school nurse an opportunity to see what effect the health status of a child has on his or her executive skills in the most important setting, the classroom.

Examples of Activities or Skills to Observe in the Classroom

It has been said that by the time a nurse even speaks to a client, 101 observations have been made. That's hyperbole of course, but the idea is that an experienced nurse can rule out some issues in minutes. When a nurse approaches a client, the nurse uses observation skills to assess many conditions: the client's mood, posture and/or orthopedic conditions, hearing, gait, sense of self-awareness, ability for self-care, attention span, eye muscle balance, skin integrity, odor, grooming, condition of clothing or lack of appropriate clothing, skin color (pale or healthy), and so on. The nurse should be familiar with normal and abnormal behaviors such as moodiness that may be temporary and mild in an adolescent or moodiness that appears excessive and disabling, a characteristic of mood disorders such as bipolar disorder.

Soft Neurological Signs for the School Nurse to Observe

Soft neurological signs can be detected through a neurological screening by the physician during a school examination or by the nurse with additional training in neurological screening. (More information on nurse-delivered neurological assessments can be found in a pediatric nursing textbook.) The neurological findings may not be obvious as gross deviations but rather very fine and potentially minor symptoms that could indicate greater significance in academics.

The school nurse may discover evidence of deficits in neurological signs during the physical assessment of the student, during classroom observation, or through discussion with the teacher. A teacher for instance may report to the team that the student wanders in class sometimes inappropriately or during lessons. If the student is unaware of such behavior or cannot explain it, that could be a sign of absence seizure also known as petit mal seizure, one that is brief and often characterized by momentary lapses of attention, or other neurological impairments that need to be evaluated. It is very important that the school nurse and teacher discuss their concerns with the parents. The student may need other medical or educational testing by the student's primary physician or other school staff, such as an occupational therapist (OT) before the IEP meeting.

The reader is referred to common pediatric textbooks for further information on how to conduct a physical assessment of the neurological system.

Visual-Motor Skills to Observe

The school nurse must observe the child in the classroom or preschool setting to help determine if the child needs further testing. Because most children can perform certain visual-motor tasks by certain ages, the school nurse should observe the child's ability to perform the following activities.

Motor skills	Age appropriate	Not apparent	Comments
Gross motor skills:			
Walks independently on straight line (by age 2)			
Alternating stair steps (by age 3)			
Hopping on either foot (by age 5)			
Standing on one foot (by age 6)			
Tandem walking—toes of back foot touching heel of front foot at each step (by age 9)			
Fine motor skills:			
Touching nose and left ear and then nose and right ear (by age 5)			
Drawing a circle (by age 3)			
Drawing a cross (by age 4)			
Drawing a square (by age 5)			
Reaching for objects within reach (by age 1)			
Drawing a triangle (by age 6)			
Preferred hand for fine motor skills (right or left)			
Strong grip on pencil or crayon?			
Visual accommodations:			
Holding pencil or crayon within normal distance to eyes (8–12 inches)			
Stacks at least 3 blocks accurately			
Strings large beads			

Checklist for the student in the classroom or natural settings.

Observation	Comment	Recommendation
Posture		
Gait		
Level of observable alertness, energy, or vitality (apparent fatigue, yawn, signs of boredom, etc.)		

Degree of participation in classroom work: independently? Needs prompts from teacher? Seeks assistance from other students? Appears engaged and attentive to teacher instructions or discussion?		
Communication (verbal, nonverbal, clarity of speech)		
Appropriate eye contact		
Physical movements: hyperactive as in frequently fidgets, frequently readjusts sitting position, taps fingers or pencils		
Social behaviors in classroom: exhibits excessive shyness, facial appearance of fearfulness, anxiety (extraordinary, excessive, and/or unwarranted worry) or sadness; cooperative, plays with others in age appropriate fashion; aggressive as in throwing objects or pushing others		
Social behaviors at play: socially active, solitary, interested, coordinated, excitable, tires easily, follows rules, takes turns, quits before game over		
If wearing glasses, in good condition?		
Grooming: clothing appears adequate for climate, in good repair, wears clothes appropriately, wears uniform if required		

Academic performance: memory, achievement, interest, reasoning, pride in performance, attitude, ability to concentrate (Ask the teacher if the child is at grade level, passing, not passing; ask the student in what subjects he thinks he does well and what he thinks he needs assistance with.)		
Perceptual status: vision, hearing, speech, evidence of understanding, concentration, excessive aversion to normal noise levels or particular sounds or lights, avoids touching or to be touched		

The above checklist is a component of the student observation for the case study evaluation (CSE). Before discussing with the parent, the nurse should discuss these findings with the classroom teacher and ask for his or her observations. If the teacher has also observed some areas of concern, the nurse should encourage the parent to take the results to the child's health care provider even before the IEP meeting.

Finally, a classroom observation is essential to really understand how the child is functioning in the classroom. The classroom teachers may share with the nurse their concerns and may provide critical missing information to complete the nurse's evaluation.

School Nurse Review of a Student's Attendance

School attendance plays an influential part in a child's education. Some students may attend every day but spend large portions of their days in the school nurse's office or other offices such as the assistant principal's office for behavioral concerns and thus miss classroom instruction. For a student with medical conditions, consider whether repeat visits represent the possibility that the student with attention deficit hyperactivity disorder (ADHD) did not take his or her morning dose of medication before school and thus the student is unable to focus in the classroom.

Similarly, a child with diabetes may be in class but due to hypoglycemia or hyperglycemia cannot function or focus well. Such instances of lack of focus may be affecting the student's overall school performance.

Also, children with multiple needs or who are medically fragile may need a one-on-one nurse to help provide daily living skills such as toileting, feeding, clearing the airway, and the like. During such times, a student may be out of the classroom or in a separate area of the classroom and thus miss some important academic instruction.

Finalizing the School Nurse's Student Evaluation Report

Once the school nurse has completed the assessments, the next step is to organize the findings in preparation for a report to the parents and the special education team at the IEP meeting to determine the student's eligibility for special education.

As previously discussed, the result of the school nurse's evaluation is a determination of whether the student's health is impacting his or her academic performance and if so, what if any nursing services are needed. When writing and before submitting the school nurse assessment report, the nurse should review whether the state dictates the content and format; most leave the content and format to the individual district and in some cases individual clinicians doing their evaluations. Any nursing protocols specific to the state or school district should be followed. Since all public school districts and state departments of education are involved in special education, nurses should first access the state department of education website to learn what optional or required forms are available. This information is often provided to school nurses, who take a state-sanctioned school nurse certification course or program or orientation.

Some nurses find it helpful to separate their findings or assessment results into objective and subjective areas. While objective and subjective findings are important and potentially enlightening, the nurse should use objective language to present his or her data and clinical assessment. When including language that offers a parent's, teacher's, or student's personal impression, this should be categorized as subjective data such as a student saying he feels stupid or a parent saying the child hates or loves school. Nurses should review health records and other school educational resources such as attendance reports, state scores, and other records.

Examples of these two categories of findings are as follows.

Findings from Objective Sources

- Student's suspension reports, injury reports, cumulative reports (including current and previous years if available), report cards, and any other important information regarding the student.
- Name and address of health care provider(s).
- Updated medical information from medical providers, which requires a medical release of information signed by parents or guardians. Always review previously recorded health data with parents for an update.

- Early intervention services (EIS) reports or individualized family service plan (IFSP) if the young child received EIS.
- School physical examination (should be recent such as within the previous school year).
- Vision and hearing screening results within twelve months of the IEP meeting. Each school district or state may have different time frames for minimum dates of physical and vision and hearing requirements.
- Medical reports from child psychiatrist and other medical specialists (cardiologist, oncologist, etc., if relevant and provided).
- A record of how much time is spent out of the classroom per day or week in the school nurse's office or elsewhere.
- Important school-related services reports requested by the school nurse such as occupational therapy (OT), physical therapy (PT), functional vision testing, and audiograms if a hearing deficit is suspected.
- Independent reports provided by parents or legal guardians.
- Results of other community systems the child has entered such as foster care or juvenile detention.

Findings from Subjective Sources—Data that Cannot Be Verified by Measurement or on Official Reports

- Interviews with the parent or the legal guardian for a current detailed health history memory or recall of prenatal history, birth events, and early child development.
- Discussions with parents about their educational concerns about the child and their perception of the student's educational strengths and weaknesses.
- Discussions with the classroom teachers about their observations of and concerns about the student.
- Nurse's observation of the student in the classroom and an interview of the student.
- How the student is functioning in the school setting.
- Student's or parents' report of friendships, enemies, or teasing and bullying issues.
- Activities of daily living (ADL) skills; student's ability for self-care.
- Sleep concerns, nightmares, access to phone, TV, and social media.
- Time spent playing video games—minutes or hours per day.
- Mobility of the family (i.e., how many schools the student has attended).
- Any recent stress or losses in the family.

Consider the Unique Needs of the Child

As mentioned earlier, each member of the IEP planning team must focus on the unique needs of the student. This concept is important when conducting evaluations as well as when presenting the report or writing up the school nursing services to be provided to the student or child.

A trap that some clinicians fall into is copying and pasting from one student's plan to another if the diagnoses or symptoms are similar. The written strengths and needs of each student should be apparent to a teacher and even to a parent of two students receiving special education; the parent should be able to determine which student the plan applies to without knowing the name of the student.

Final Steps in Writing the School Nurse Report

At this point in the process, some school nurses will include information about relevant nursing diagnoses that may be a part of the nursing process and are clinical judgments about individual, family, or community experiences and responses to actual or potential health problems and life processes. If these are included, the school nurse should make sure the entire team (parent, student, school administrators, teachers, and other clinical specialists at the IEP meeting) are aware of the term *nursing diagnosis* as opposed to the term *medical diagnosis* and make sure that the language of the nursing diagnosis is understandable to all.

Whether or not nursing diagnoses are included, the final step before the IEP eligibility meeting is for the nurse to review the information and determine if in his or her professional opinion and based on the totality of the health evaluation that the student's academic difficulties are or are not likely related to past or current health issues. If the answer is yes, the nurse should recommend how the health issues can be addressed to remove or mitigate their effects on the student's learning process.

SECTION 3

The Special Education Meeting

CHAPTER 5

The School Nurse and Eligibility Determination Conference (EDC)

The school nurse who has participated in the process from referral and domain meeting to the performance of the evaluations and has organized his or her findings and interpretations of those findings will be ready to present the school nurse report to the IEP team at the eligibility determination conference (EDC).

To be eligible for special education, a student must meet certain eligibility conditions established by federal law.[10] The EDC will determine whether the child is eligible for special education; if so, a meeting to develop the IEP will follow. If the evaluation determines that the student does not meet the criteria for eligibility for special education, the meeting concludes. Any team member including parents can write a rebuttal, and there are times when the decision not to qualify a student for special education results in a request for a hearing. However, the due process hearing is not within the scope of this book. As summarized by Johns (2016, 8), a "parent may contest a school's decision, and a due process hearing can occur when laws and regulations leave some questions unanswered or there is a controversy and disagreement about what should and should not be provided by the school districts." The school nurse who has participated in a student's special education evaluation that is now involved in due process is referred to books such as the one mentioned in this footnote.[11]

Nurses who attend an EDC might feel intimidated if they have not established informal relationships with other team members and little collaboration has occurred. It may be helpful for novice school nurses to sit with the team members they are most comfortable with to gain the confidence necessary to speak authoritatively about the domain. An EDC is also possibly the first

[10] 71 FR 46753, Aug. 14, 2006, as amended at 72 FR 61307, Oct. 30, 2007; 82 FR 29761, June 30, 2017; see appendix I for the list of eligible disabilities.

[11] Beverley H. Johns, *Your Classroom Guide to Special Education Law* (Baltimore: Brooks Publishing, 2016). Information about a webinar by the author is available at https://home.edweb.net/webinar/every-educator-know-special-education-law/.

opportunity for the parents and the other IEP team members to understand the role of the school nurse in this process. Through nursing assessments including classroom observation, the nurse will develop a plan to support the child's right to have a safe school environment.

Parents should be active participants in the IEP meeting and understand the school team's findings. To this end, school nurses must be mindful not to talk in acronyms or explain them as necessary and define all terminology so the parents and others who might not be familiar with it can understand it.

The EDC Meeting to Determine Eligibility for Special Education

Parents and other team members receive the agenda for the EDC meeting, which is led by the school staff. The participants include the student's parents or guardians who as active members provide critical input for evaluating the student, the IEP team, the classroom teacher, and other key support staff as needed.

Students of any age may attend the meeting and should attend if they are older than fourteen and a half. The older the student, the more he or she needs to learn to and practice advocating for his or her learning and personal needs. Students who learn to advocate for themselves may be more successful in the IEP as they transition from high school to college or work.

During the EDC Meeting

- The school case manager or designee will introduce each team member to the parents and state his or her role in the school. The IEP staff and parents will sign a cover sheet confirming their attendance.
- All written evaluation reports including the school nurse's must be presented to the parents/guardians for review at the eligibility conference.
- The IEP team members will present summaries of their assessments to the parents and their colleagues. The school nurse will discuss the health findings and in summary confirm with the IEP team and parents the presence or absence of any health issues past or current that could affect the student's learning.
- Parents (and student if present) may question each evaluator including the school nurse about the reports or may add more-detailed information.
- Team members should describe as many positive attributes and good behaviors of the student as possible and celebrate their successes minor or major.

The IEP team including the school nurse develops a written summary of the evaluation results and considers all available information to determine if the child qualifies for special education services. The parents and team members discuss the findings and determine if an individualized education program (IEP) is indicated. If any team member including the parent does not agree with the majority decision, he or she might not sign the separate consent form for services and will generally provide a written dissenting report.

At the EDC meeting, the school nurse should be present to give the report and listen to the findings of the other team members, support the parents and the child, and be an active member of the IEP team. From time to time, there may be urgent circumstances for which the nurse or another team member may need to be excused from the IEP meeting. If any member of the team—in this example the nurse—is excused, the parents or guardians must be notified of the excusal; the meeting can still be held if the parent agrees to or permits the excusal. Whether in attendance or not, the nurse provides a written report that is turned in to the IEP team or entered by the nurse into an electronic format for inclusion in the report. However, if the student has health concerns and the nurse cannot be present, the team should consider rescheduling the meeting.

The school nurse must be prepared to discuss and share the important health and medical findings from the school nurse report with the parents and the IEP team during the EDC. It is very important to discuss how the student with medical issues is functioning in school. The parents and the IEP team will determine if the current medical findings and any other medical reports suggest that the student is eligible for special education or any school nursing services.

At this meeting, the school nurse should be prepared to listen to and understand the terminology and purpose of reports from other team members. For example, the term *executive function* (EF) may be used by the school psychologist, who usually does a variety of tests addressing how the child learns. In an email to the authors on March 25, 2019, school psychologist Lynda Stone, PhD, described executive functioning (EF) skills and competence that include "emotional regulation control, attending control, mental planning, task initiative, transition, goal directed, impulse control, working memory, self-monitoring, time management, and organization."

Executive functioning (EF) includes the mental processes and skills required to learn and retain learning. The school nurse must have a working knowledge of EF to understand how the student is learning in the classroom, the student's behavior, and description of activities in which the student is participating in the classroom. Is the student learning, paying attention, and completing tasks in class? Does the student need prompts, suggestions, hints, or nonverbal signals to help stay on task?

It is important to keep EF skills in mind during the school nurse report and analyze the potential effect health concerns can have on learning. Students need verbal and nonverbal communication skills; if they have deficits in vision or hearing, their verbal skills and their ability to provide full executive functioning will be limited. Students with poor dental care and oral health issues may find it difficult to function in skills that require oral communication. If students have poor posture due to muscle flaccidity or other orthopedic issues, nonverbal communication can be limited and may be misinterpreted as a lack of interest or attention or even respect.

In addressing the student's or child's unique needs at the EDC meeting, the school nurse should reflect on the findings included in the written assessment and be prepared to address with the parents and IEP team members points of discussion such as these:

- Are the student's health issues impacting his or her classroom learning?
- Does the child need to see the school nurse or related support staff to be successful in school? Does the school nurse not need to see the student at all because no health issues are impacting student's learning?
- If the student needs nursing services for anything other than routine care, would the student be successful and function well in school? Examples are medication, medical treatment, one-on-one nursing services, and special procedures such as tracheal suctioning, catheterizations, gastrostomy tube feedings, and other treatments.
- If the student needs nursing services that must be provided by a nurse at a certain level of nursing licensure or can be provided by other personnel. Prior to offering or delegating any nursing services, school nurses should clearly understand the scope and stipulations of the Nurse Practice Act (NPA) in their states. Only a nurse using professional nursing judgment and with a clear understanding of the state NPA can legally determine if a health care task can be delegated and if so the skill level required for someone else to carry out that delegated activity.

Key Terms to Understand the Impact of a Student's Health on Learning

IEP team members often use different terms to explain a student's current academic performance and the issues that are impacting his or her learning. The nurse should be familiar with the terms in the following paragraph, which are often used interchangeably to mean Present Level of Academic Achievement and Functional Performance (PLAAFP). As of the date of this book, the terms PLAAFP and impact statement are most relevant to understand when presenting student's health findings related to educational impact in learning at the IEP meeting for the student.

PLAAFP

Under IDEA 2004, the IEP must include a statement of the child's current levels of academic achievement and functional performance. This statement is sometimes referred to as present levels or with older terms, PLOP, present levels of performance, or PLEP, present levels of educational performance. The current term as of this publication is PLAAFP. The PLAAFP is the first written statement in the IEP plan documentation of the child's ability and current achievement at the time the IEP is written.

Noted special education attorney Pete Wright and psychotherapist Pam Wright describe PLAAFP as

> objective data that describe what your child knows and is able to do. They describe your child's strengths, challenges, and needs. The present levels include baseline data. The term "performance" describes what your child can do. The Present Levels describe your child's unique needs that result from his disability. The Present Levels are the foundation for everything else in the IEP. Present Levels of academic achievement include subjects like reading, math, and spelling. Present Levels of functional performance include non-academic and functional areas like communication, fine motor skills, behavior and social skills, and daily life activities. (Wrightslaw.com 2019)

Impact Statement

Some IEP teams will refer to the PLAAFP as the impact statement. More accurately, the PLAAFP forms a basis for the impact statement. While the PLAAFP describes strengths and needs, the impact statement answers the question of how the child's disability affects (impacts) his or her involvement and progress in the general curriculum. At this point, the school nurse will identify the student's areas of need in terms of health, vision, and hearing in relation to the student's performance if it is significantly and consistently below the performance of similar grade (academic achievement) and age (functional performance) peers as a result of the disability.

If the school IEP team and the parents are concerned about the child's behavior in the classroom, the school psychologist, classroom teacher, or social worker may do a behavior rating inventory to assess how the child's behavior may be interfering with the executive function (EF) in school. The school nurse must understand the assessments performed by other team members to get the whole picture of the child in the classroom.

The assessments of the classroom teacher, school psychologist, parents, nurse, social worker, speech-language pathologist, occupational therapist (OT), and physical therapist (PT) if performed provide a better understanding of why the child may not be learning, and they will help develop and solidify numerous interventions strategies for the child in the classroom.

It is very important that the nurse shares in and understands the information from other IEP members including their perspectives based on their observations of the student in the classroom or a different but natural setting for a child.

The school nurse must understand the relationships between all the data and refer to the domains in the area of health, vision, and hearing to understand if problems in those areas cause an adverse effect, or even a supportive effect, or bear any relationship to the student's learning. The school nurse must understand the specific skills and activities the student will be taught to improve his or her academic performance.

The evaluation reports may be handwritten, typed up, or entered into a computer special education online form or program at school. The school nurse will write, submit, and orally report a school nurse summary with key factors to share with IEP team members and parents at the EDC. The report should be brief but cover the necessary information. For example, a normal vaginal delivery of a baby at term with weight and size within normal limits and no complications can be simply stated exactly with those words without recreating the birth scene. A birth that was complicated with potential deprivation of oxygen may be lengthier with a note to those at the meeting: "The birth history was complicated and may have impacted future brain development due to …"

The school nurse summary is written in the health summary on the student's school nurse assessment form or the IEP web-based management system. It should be brief but should include the following points:

- mother's pregnancy condition and pertinent prenatal history and birth weight
- date of last current medical examination and other important medical reports
- status of immunizations;
- height, weight, and body mass index
- vision and hearing results within a year of the meeting
- current and past medications taken and for what reasons
- any past or current medical conditions possibly affecting the student's learning

Whenever possible, school nurses should identify and support the good health behaviors the student demonstrates and presumably the parents had instituted. As discussed, any positive reinforcement may be welcome by a family that is learning mostly about the deficits or weaknesses of a student.

Examples of the School Nurse Written or Oral Summary Section at the EDC

The following examples show summaries of school nursing assessments.

Student 1

Student is three-year-old male who was referred for an initial case study evaluation (CSE) due to possible developmental delay (DD) in all areas. Mother was the informant for the interview. This child is the youngest of four children. Mother is thirty. She did not seek prenatal care until the last trimester. Weight gain for mother was twenty pounds. Student was premature; normal vaginal delivery at seven months gestation at St. Francis Hospital and weighed two pounds, four ounces. Placed in neonatal ICU for two months. Student had difficulty sucking and gaining weight.

Was discharged at five pounds after two months in St. Francis. Mother stated child did gain weight but slowly. At six months, the child was enrolled in early interventions services (EIS) because of poor muscle tone. Student received occupational therapy (OT), physical therapy (PT), and speech therapy at the hospital and home. Milestones appeared delayed; walked at two years, now starting to talk, saying two words together. Student not toilet trained. Appetite poor; able to eat with assistance. Student developed seizures at age two; on daily medication. Needs medication during a.m. in school.

Last medical exam on file June 2018 stating development delay and seizure disorder (grand mal). Neurological findings: poor muscle tone, hypotonic. Height and weight below 50 percent. Immunizations are up to date. Vision and hearing screening were unable to be obtained; referred to clinic for more testing.

An individual health care plan (IHCP) and emergency care plan (ECP) is on file for seizure disorder. Student may need one-on-one assistance with self-care including toileting.

In summary, it appears this preschooler's previous and current medical condition is having an impact on his physical development and he is at risk for later delays in academic and functional performance. Recommend the school nurse provide services daily for fifteen minutes for medication and monitor the medical follow-up for seizure disorders and vision and hearing referrals.

Student 2

Student is ten-year-old female referred for initial case study evaluation (CSE) due to poor academic success in math and reading. She appears to be behind more than two years in these academic areas. Conference with mother to obtain history revealed mother was twenty-three during the pregnancy and prenatal care began during the first semester. There were no medical concerns during the pregnancy, and student was born full term after normal vaginal delivery at Throop Hospital. Birth weight seven pounds ten ounces with no postnatal problems. Home with mother after two days in the hospital.

During the first year, weight tripled, had a good appetite, no serious illness or surgery during the first year or later. Developmental milestones appeared normal. No history of vision or hearing problems. Last medical exam 12/2018 with normal physical findings. Vision and hearing screening passed 12/2018. At this time, it appears that no adverse effect from health is impacting the student's school performance. Thus, no specialized school nursing services at this time will be provided for the student.

Age of Majority

The term age of majority generally refers to when a young person reaches the age at which one is legally considered an adult. Most states consider eighteen as the age of majority. Students of age should know that their rights are being transferred from their parents to themselves during the IEP meeting, and they should receive verbal notification that at that point they are in control of their educational rights and perhaps other rights such as those to make medical decisions on their own behalf. This notification may involve written verification that the student had had his or her rights explained. Some districts may have a pamphlet or other written information available for the student to sign and keep. However, a student who reaches the age of majority may have his or her status as an independent legally withheld and instead maintained by a parent or other guardian due to his or her disability. If this is done, the parent or guardian should produce the legal documentation of that action.

Conclusion of EDC Meeting

It is required that at least the majority of the IEP team, including parent, consent to the conclusions of the evaluation and determination of disability and placement in special education and related or support services. Most important is the agreement or disagreement of the parents. The parents or legal guardians will consent or formally dissent from the identified disability and the program and sign (or formally decline to sign) the eligibility forms.

If the parents or any other team member does not agree with the findings and/or the recommendations, the parents as well as any team members may provide a statement in support of their disagreement. If the school does not agree, the parents may request mediation, a process whereby a neutral party may help resolve the disagreement, or they may request due process, the legal steps and processes that protect the rights of students with disabilities to address their concerns.

If a determination is made that a child has a disability and needs special education and related services, an IEP must be developed for the child in accordance with federal regulations. The IEP development takes place at the IEP meeting. The IEP meeting has two general purposes: to establish measurable, annual, academic goals for the child and to state the special education, related services, and supplementary aids and services the public agency will provide to or on behalf of the child.

When constructing an appropriate educational program for a child with a disability, the IEP team broadly considers the child's involvement and participation in these three main areas of school life:

- the general education curriculum, meaning the subject matter provided to children without disabilities and the associated skills they are expected to develop and apply
- extracurricular activities
- nonacademic activities[12]

The IEP team including parents and student if present then moves into the IEP development meeting. This may take place at the same time and place as the eligibility conference or later at a mutually agreed upon time.

[12] Extracurricular activities and nonacademic activities refer to school activities that fall outside the realm of the general curriculum. These are usually voluntary and tend to be social, special interest, or athletic but may also be academic. They typically involve others of the same age and may be organized and guided by teachers or other school personnel. Examples are yearbook, school newspaper, school sports, school clubs, academic competitions, lunch, recess, band, pep rallies, assemblies, field trips, after-school programs, and recreational clubs.

CHAPTER 6

Development of the Individual Education Program (IEP)

At the conclusion of the eligibility determination conference (EDC), a report is written relevant to the decision about the child's eligibility. This meeting report must include signatures of the participants indicating their presence at the meeting and any written statement provided by a participant who wishes to be on record as disagreeing with the conclusions expressed in the team's report.

If the conclusion is that the student or child is eligible for special education services (IEP), these key points should be reviewed as most of them are written in IDEA regulations as required. These requirements are paraphrased below and will be discussed further in this chapter and others.

- Because the IEP can be understood as the blueprint or program and a legally binding contract for the special education experiences of a child with a disability across all school settings academic and extracurricular, the members of a child's IEP team must be sure the resulting IEP contains the specific information required by IDEA 2004.
- In most cases, if the student is determined eligible, the IEP development meeting occurs immediately following the EDC meeting. If any participant will not be writing a section on the IEP or provided relating services, he or she may be excused at the end of the EDC and before the IEP development meeting.
- The case manager will ask the parents their concerns about their child's learning per IDEA 2004 and will write these concerns on the IEP document for the IEP team to discuss and address the means to support the child in learning.
- A statement of the child's present levels of academic achievement and functional performance (PLAAFP) including how the child's disability affects his or her involvement and progress in the general education curriculum.
- A statement of the special education and related services and supplementary aids and services to be provided to or on behalf of the child.

- The IEP team including parents then discuss the student's educational needs and recommend the appropriate educational program.
- The related services staff will then discuss the student's functional needs and recommend the appropriate plans to address those needs.
- The IEP team including related services staff if relevant must write the specific services required on the legal document, or the PLAAFP (discussed further in this chapter).
- If the school nurse, the IEP team, and the parents of the student agree that nursing services are needed, the parents will sign consent forms for the services just as for other support staff services such as speech and social work services. It is a good idea to also obtain a consent for release of information between the student's health care provider and the school nurse if not already obtained.
- Parents receive copies of all IEP documents. Upon completion of the IEP meeting, the district must provide a copy of the IEP that documents the determination of eligibility to the parent(s). A copy of that IEP shall be kept locked as with other student records and filed with the student's cumulative record. District policy about the storage and security of special education files should be observed.
- Once the parent signs the IEP in agreement with the plan, the student services personnel who are named in the plan have obtained written parental/guardian consent to provide the listed services.
- After the IEP team determines the student's unique educational needs with the written IEP and related services, the IEP team determines an educational setting in which the student's IEP can be provided in the least restrictive environment (LRE), an educational setting for exceptional students and students with disabilities that minimizes their exclusion from students without disabilities. LRE placement of students with special needs promotes the maximum possible interaction with the general school population.
- If the student is covered by Medicaid or other similar public health insurance and the school participates in Medicaid reimbursement, parents need to be aware of the services, and the school may ask the parents to provide a Medicaid number and sign consent for the services provided so the school can receive state reimbursement for them.
- A statement of the program modifications or support of school personnel that will enable the child to advance appropriately toward annual goals, make progress in the general education curriculum, participate in extracurricular and other nonacademic activities, and be educated and participate with other children with and without disabilities.
- An explanation of the extent if any to which the child will not participate with nondisabled children in regular classes and extracurricular and nonacademic activities.
- A statement of any individual accommodations necessary to measure the academic achievement and functional performance of the child on state- and district-wide assessments.

Note: If the IEP team determines that the child must take an alternate assessment instead of a regular, state- or district-wide assessment of student achievement, the IEP must include a statement explaining why the child cannot participate in the regular assessment and why the particular alternate assessment selected is appropriate for the child.

- The projected date for the beginning of the services and modifications and the anticipated frequency, location, and duration of those services and modifications.
- Changes in the formal disabilities on the IEP form cannot be made without holding another IEP meeting. However, if there is no change in the overall amount of service, some adjustments in the scheduling of services may be possible without another IEP meeting.
- The IEPs of most students with special needs will be linked to the learning standards with individualized approaches to the depth and timetables for achievement. For students with severe and profound disabilities, few of these standards may apply in terms of achievement, but the standards can still serve as a target. (US Department of Education 2019)

Related Services/Specialized Instructional Support Personnel (SISP)

Once a student's disability has been identified and eligibility has been established, the plan for supporting the student's educational needs must be developed. It is then that the team determines the need for related services. IDEA 2004 defines related services as

> transportation and such developmental, corrective, and other supportive services as are required to assist a child with a disability to benefit from special education, and includes speech language pathology and audiology services, interpreting services, psychological services, physical and occupational therapy, recreation, including therapeutic recreation, early identification and assessment of disabilities in children, counseling services, including rehabilitation counseling, orientation and mobility services, and medical services for diagnostic or evaluation purposes. Related services also include school health services and school nurse services, social work services in schools, and parent counseling and training. (US Congress 2004)

The law further defines *school health services* and *school nurse services* as health services designed to enable a child with a disability to receive free appropriate public education (FAPE) as described in the child's IEP. School nurse services are services provided by a qualified school nurse. School health services are services that may be provided by a qualified school nurse or other qualified person. The use of one term over the other depends in large part on the scope of work in your state's health care licensing laws and delegation rules of your state's Nurse Practice Act.

Federal regulations allow individual states to determine the credentials required of the student services personnel. For example, in some states, a school nurse or other service provider must hold state certification; in others, it must be national certification; and in others, a master's degree is required. Still others require no credentials beyond a professional license. It is thus important for nurses to learn and follow their state's rules.

The list of related services is not exhaustive and may include other developmental, corrective, or support services if they are required to assist a child with a disability to benefit from special education. Examples include artistic and cultural programs, art, music, and dance therapy.

Excluded Related Services

Certain types of student support equipment and its maintenance are not considered part of related services, so districts are not responsible for providing or replacing them. In the case of health, these are usually implanted devices. IDEA makes a specific exception to the list of related services: surgically implanted devices including cochlear implants are not related services. This exception is new with IDEA 2004 and shows the advance of time and technology.

Cochlear implants are not the only surgically implanted devices that are not considered related services; others include insulin pumps, baclofen pumps, pacemakers, G-tubes, and vagus nerve stimulator devices. Although school staff may use the equipment and check its maintenance, the school is not obligated or expected to provide the equipment.

However, if a child has a surgically implanted device, the scope of the public agency's responsibility to provide supportive, related services in relation to that device is covered in IDEA. Public agencies are not responsible for optimizing, maintaining, or replacing such devices. For example, a school district is not responsible for the medical care of a G-tube such as the placement or care for a complication, but the school district is responsible for administering G-tube feedings because a child must receive nutrition in order to learn.

While public agencies are not responsible for mapping a cochlear implant, they do have a role to play in providing services and supports to help children with cochlear implants.

Public agencies are responsible for "routine checking to determine if the external component of a surgically implanted device is turned on and working" (71 Fed. Reg. 46570) and for providing other types of services the child needs as determined by the IEP team, including these:

- assistive technology (AT) (e.g., an FM system)
- proper classroom acoustical modifications
- educational support services (e.g., educational interpreters)
- receiving related services (e.g., speech and language services) necessary for the child to benefit from special education services. (US Department of Education CFR 2016)

Transition Planning for Students with Medical Issues

IDEA requires that by age sixteen, the student has a transition plan, a plan and services to transition into adulthood and wherever possible to learn to manage employment, transportation, self-care, and other responsibilities of adulthood. Some states require transition plans as early as age fourteen or younger if deemed appropriate by the IEP team.

It is important for the school nurse to attend IEP meetings when students have medical issues that need to be addressed during the transition planning. Transition plans are so important because the goal is to maximize lifelong abilities and through appropriate health care services that continue as the student moves from either adolescence to adulthood or from one school to another. For the student eligible for transition service planning, the school nurse will consider a student's goal related to transitioning of health care.

Students who will have a transition plan may be expected to demonstrate meeting IEP goals by participating in authentic assessment such as role-playing and encounters that are part of the student's activities of daily life. This performance-based assessment technique is based on the student's application of knowledge to real-life activities, real-world settings, or a simulation of such settings using real-life, real-world activities.

Developing the IEP: Begin with Writing PLAAFP

Developing the IEP (written program) begins with the writing of the PLAAFP, the first written statement in the IEP documenting the child's ability and current achievement at the time the IEP is written. The PLAAFP may be considered the basis for the rest of the IEP. For the school nurse who is involved in developing the health-related issues in the IEP, the following procedure is expected.

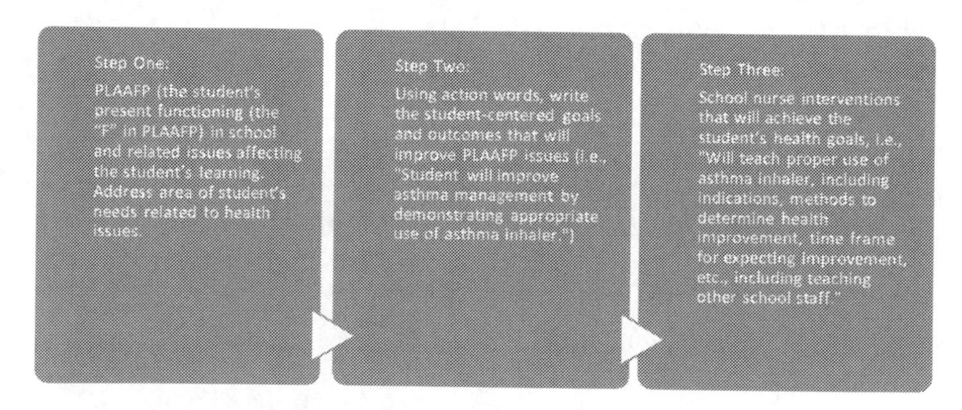

Flow chart of PLAAFP and student's IEP goal. © Copyright 2019 by authors

Step One: Write PLAAFP Section on the IEP Form

The PLAAFP is a summary of information and data about what the student currently knows and is able to do in the following areas:

- communication
- academic performance
- health, vision, hearing
- social/emotional status
- general intelligence
- motor abilities

Some key points for the school nurse to understand before writing the PLAAFP include these.

- The PLAAFP is a written, concise, narrative summary (baseline) that indicates how the known disability is affecting the student's academic and functional work in the school setting.
- It is a narrative picture of the student in the classroom and description of the student's learning compared to his or her peers there; could someone who does not know the student read the PLAAFP and get a good idea of his or her functioning in the classroom?

The school nurse is responsible for writing the PLAAFP based on IDEA 2004 if a health issue is impacting the student's learning. In that case, the PLAAFP must include statements about those issues and how they are related to the student's academic and/or function performance. If there is no health issue impacting learning, the nurse is not involved in writing the PLAAFP.

To write a PLAAFP, nurses should understand that "present levels of academic achievement" refers to how a student is performing in the general education curriculum. For preschoolers, performance levels may include pre-academic readiness skills. Documentation should reflect the results of the most recent evaluation in the PLAAFP. Functional performance is related to activities associated with activities of daily living (ADL), the skills necessary for the child or student to live at his or her age, which include actions in the categories of health/physical, social/emotional, independent functions, motor skills, and so on. The nurse may consider the functional performance of students with conditions such as attention deficit hyperactivity disorder (ADHD), asthma, cancer, depression, and hospitalizations of any kind or temporary or chronic health conditions that are often causes of learning difficulties if they qualified for an IEP.

The following data should also guide the nurse's development of the PLAAFP. The list is not exhaustive; rather, it serves as a prompt to identify current educational performance in writing the student's PLAAFP. It should include the student's record in these areas:

- attendance
- passing grades
- struggling in the classroom
- history of retention
- behavior in school
- incidences of bullying or being bullied

While not all concerns will apply to every student, nurses may add their own questions to the PLAAFP to demonstrate how medical issues or disabilities impact the student's learning in the classroom.

Example of a Written PLAAFP

Student is ten-year male in fifth grade diagnosed with attention deficit hyperactivity disorder (ADHD) last year and currently on prescription medication to treat the disorder. In the classroom, student is falling behind in his classwork because of his inability to pay attention and stay on task. Student has difficulty following two-step verbal instructions. He is at times unprepared with his homework. Student needs medication to help him focus. Medication will be given at noon in school. Last medical exam on file states medical diagnosis of ADHD. Student did pass vision and hearing screening 12/2017.

With the description above of a PLAAFP, one should be able to visualize the student in the classroom. If the nurse does not have a mental picture of the student yet, continue describing the student, specifically, how the student is showing that he or she is learning and functioning in the classroom. Once the nurse understands the student from his or her health presentation and academic presentation, the nurse will have transitioned from a nurse with a solely clinical focus to a school nurse in the comprehensive role of a nurse who serves students with IEPs.

Behavioral Intervention Plan

Some students with an IEP will be determined to need a behavior intervention plan (BIP), a written plan used to address problem behavior that includes positive behavioral interventions, strategies, and support. It is required under IDEA (https://idea.ed.gov) when the local education agency (school or district), the parent, and the relevant members of the child's IEP team determine that a student's misconduct was a manifestation of his or her disability. A BIP is also required in the IEP when the IEP team has decided that a child with a disability demonstrates behaviors that impede his or her learning or that of others.

Most school nurses will not write a BIP but may participate in its creation. For example, if a student with a behavioral issue comes to the nurse for service such as a playground injury, the nurse should know if there is a BIP and what the plan is to control the behavior. Otherwise, the nurse may be inadvertently defeating the BIP or at least not handling the situation appropriately.

When an IEP team determines that a BIP is necessary, the team members should use information about the targeted behavior's function gathered from the functional behavioral assessment. The IEP team should include strategies to teach the student more-acceptable ways to get what he or she wants or needs, to decrease future occurrences of the targeted behavior, and to address any repeated episodes of the targeted behavior. Typically, the behavioral intervention plan will not consist of simply one intervention; rather, it will be a plan with several interventions designed to address the targeted behavior.

Step Two: Writing the Student-Centered Health Goals and Outcomes in the IEP

The 2019 US Department of Education's IDEA regulation 300.320(a)(4) stipulates that each child's IEP must contain these items.

> A statement of the special education and related services and supplementary aids and services based on peer-reviewed research to the extent practicable to be provided to the child, or on behalf of the child, and a statement of the program modifications or supports for school personnel that will be provided to enable the child—
>
> 1. To advance appropriately toward attaining the annual goals;
> 2. To be involved in and make progress in the general education curriculum in accordance with paragraph (a)(1) of this section, and to participate in extracurricular and other nonacademic activities; and
> 3. To be educated and participate with other children with disabilities and non-disabled children in the activities described in this section … [§300.320(a)(4)]
>
>   a. A statement of measurable annual goals, describing estimated yearly (academic year) outcomes for a student with a disability. Annual goals address areas of identified needs and include both academic and functional goals.[13]

[13] The performance measure for setting the student's goals may be compared to an age equivalent, comparing students of similar age, or a grade equivalent (GE), comparing students in same grade. A nurse-written goal should also take into account the student's equivalency in terms of the physical or cognitive deficits that may be present recognizing that the norms of normally developing or typically developing children may be different with disabled children.

4. A description of how the child's progress toward meeting the annual goals will be measured, using skills found in daily activities where appropriate, and when periodic progress reports will be provided. (US Department of Education 2019)

The IEP is a legally binding contract. Each service to be provided and each annual goal to be addressed is a written commitment for the delivery of services to meet a student's educational needs. No direct, related, or support services written in the IEP to be provided by the public school or school district can be at any cost to the parent; that would violate federal free appropriate public education (FAPE) law.

Based on school or state policy, all instructional support school personnel staff may write a student's IEP annual goal related to the state's learning standards and the scope of the practitioner's practice. This means that the speech therapist will write annual goals for the student's communication and speech issues and that the social worker will do the same for emotional or behavioral disorders. The classroom teacher and/or special education teacher will write academic goals and accommodations for the student. The school nurse or other licensed health care provider will provide annual goals based on the nursing or health services to be provided. Though the position (social worker, speech pathologist, RN, LPN, unlicensed assistant, etc.) is listed as the provider, the name of the provider (whether teacher, medical, or other) should not be used to prevent the need to revise the IEP should that staff member leave a position or a substitute needs to provide the service.

The nurse usually writes annual goals limited to health functioning; these goals reflect the nurse's best interventions for removing the health condition that is affecting learning (such as vision correction lenses) or ameliorating the condition (such as improving nighttime symptoms of severe asthma). The goal is not a nursing goal but a student goal to maintain skin integrity through interventions such as frequent repositioning in a wheelchair to avoid the student's developing sores.

If an academic goal is relevant to health, a health related goal may be appropriate. For example, if a student needs to see the school nurse daily for medication, the nurse should consider writing an IEP goal based on the state health education learning standards, i.e., self-care, health promotion, and so on. If a student with an IEP has mild asthma, the nurse can visit the student quarterly to discuss the current asthma management procedures if the asthma is affecting the student's ability to learn. If the asthma is not impacting the student's learning, the student's school nurse needs are still met and recorded as a related service in the plan, but a student goal will likely not be written.

The annual goals must be achievable and realistic for the student in light of his or her developmental age and ability to comprehend or achieve the goals. With the student at the center, the goals must reflect SMART goal language, e.g., specific, measurable, attainable, realistic/relevant, and time bound.

When writing such goals, it is recommended per IDEA 2004 to write goals based on peer-reviewed research and implement such research-based practices or evidence-based practices (EBP) whenever possible by identifying practices supported by rigorous evidence of success in meeting goals (US Department of Education 2019).

School nurses may inadvertently fall back on the research that was available when they were in nursing school, but subsequent research can provide evidence that may change their practices.

Consider these scenarios of when new research on EBP might be indicated:

- What is the current EBP for case management for student with attention deficit hyperactivity disorder (ADHD)? Are medications other than the traditional methylphenidate indicated? Is behavioral intervention alone effective? If so, how often should it be delivered? Are newer medications delivered transdermally more effective or more likely to be accepted by the student? Answers to these questions might require some research before a nurse can create a nursing care plan and goals for the student.
- What is the current EBP for treating a student with severe allergies and a specific learning disability (SLD)? Does the current EBP treatment guideline call for use of an antihistamine and a waiting period before a more severe reaction occurs? Do current guidelines call for immediate use of epinephrine in a student with a history of anaphylaxis? Using EBP would be necessary before a nurse challenges a physician order if necessary. (School nurses can research other topics with EBP guidelines at https://www.ahrq.gov/gam/index.html.)

Guidance on Writing Student Health Outcomes

The school nurse who is providing services to a student who qualifies for an IEP should be prepared to write at least one student IEP goal with anticipated outcomes that will address the student's health problems that are affecting his or her ability to learn. To reiterate a very important point, the student's IEP goal is student centered and in the realm of the nurse related to health with the ultimate goal of improving academic achievement. It should be written to determine the student's level of self-care as he or she develops into adolescence.

Just as the student's goals should be written on the school's IEP goal sheet, they should be written and included in the IEP. On average, a student would not need more than one or two goals to address his or her health condition. Remember that the IEP goal is a written commitment for the delivery of services to meet a student's educational needs. A school district must ensure that all the related services specified in the IEP including the amount of time for those services are provided to a student.

The Connection between the PLAAFP and IEP Health Goal to Address the Student's Health Issue That Is Impacting Learning

Consider a student who has severe diabetes, an eligible condition under the classification of other health impairment (OHI) if the impairment is affecting the student's learning.

- The PLAAFP has determined that this student's health condition (diabetes) is impacting learning because
    - the student is not compliant with self-care and/or the student's diabetes is brittle (unpredictable swings in blood glucose levels), and/or
    - the student is missing school time either by remaining at home or being out of class for diabetes management a large percentage of the day, and/or
    - the student is exhibiting physical or mental fatigue and does not fully participate in classroom instruction.

- Annual IEP goal 1: (addressing the area of need to improve PLAAFP): Student will come to the nurse's office daily to improve diabetic care management and to discuss breakfast intake and carbohydrate plans for lunch.
- Annual IEP goal 2: Student will come to the nurse's office daily to discuss and calculate the amount of insulin to be given at school at lunch. Student will write amount of insulin on log to monitor daily care.

An annual IEP goal must be meaningful and measurable. It needs to be monitored to determine if it is helping the student progress in the general curriculum. It is important to measure the student's progress as the student benefits from the support of the school nurse services and to present a progress report, an evaluation, to the IEP team and the parents.

The school nurse provides the classroom teacher a summary of the student's progress to include in the report card in addition to the IEP progress report. On the IEP report card, the school nurse describes the student's progress toward the student's IEP goals each grading period or semester. Though the school nurse would be communicating more frequently with the family about the child's condition in school, report cards show if the student is making progress toward the IEP goals. If not, the IEP team needs to review the goal and possibly change it or adopt a new goal to better support the student.

Annual goals are statements that identify what knowledge, skills, and behavior a student is expected to demonstrate before the next scheduled meeting, usually one school year from the current IEP meeting, with periodic evaluations similar to grading periods for students in the general education program.

Referring to the example of a student learning to manage diabetes, consider if the student's IEP goal includes improving his or her diabetic condition; improvement in diabetes management may transfer over and improve his or her ability to learn in the classroom.

When appropriate, nurses should link student goals related to health services to health education or other curricular lessons. Most school districts teach health in the school curriculum. The school district may include this in the IEP; in Illinois, the learning standard most relevant is 22A, Health Promotion, Prevention and Treatment. In Washington State, a similar learning standard is phrased as Standard 6: "Students will demonstrate the ability to use goal-setting skills to enhance health" (State of Washington, Office of Superintendent of Public Instruction 2019). North Carolina has a learning standard about nutrition, 4.NP.1.

The nurse should plan healthy nutrition and fitness routines as appropriate for a student with a mental health disorder or anorexia nervosa that has contributed to difficulty in learning.

Components of a Measurable Annual Goal

To properly measure a student's achievement of annual IEP goals, the nurse will need to determine what criteria and procedures will be used to evaluate goal achievement and the student's progress. The goal for an immobile client might be to maintain skin integrity; the achievement would be that the client's skin is intact without redness or breakdown, which would be verified by the nurse's inspecting the skin daily during morning care.

After writing the general annual IEP goal, nurses need to establish benchmarks, short-term objectives, increments of the student's learning that demonstrate progress toward the annual goal. They also include time limits with a quarterly report card to show progress during that time. The benchmarks are stepping-stones to help a student make progress.

The benchmarks address what individual or repeated steps the student needs to take to reach his or her IEP goals. What the student does must be measurable so that the school nurse can count, observe, and document the student's progress each quarter.

Evaluation Criteria

The evaluation criteria define how well over time the nurse needs to measure or see the student's movement toward the annual IEP goal. The goal is usually described in terms of degree of accuracy, the extent to which a student's academic performance or response to the goal is without significant errors. School districts use different methods of evaluation criteria such as a percentage increase or decrease, a certain number of correct responses out of attempts, or other methods. Nurses should follow their school's measurement criteria.

Many districts encourage school staff to begin with a present, achievable number, encourage progress, and move progressively toward a higher achievement level. For example, if a student currently completes proper inhaler use a third of the time; begin with a measure that is one out of three for first grading period in terms of inhaler use, two out of three by the end of the second grading period, and three out of three by the end of the year. For a student dealing with anorexia who normally eats only a quarter of a meal, begin with consuming a quarter of her lunch and work toward consuming 90 percent of what is served and is reasonably expected to be consumed.

It may take more than one school year for a student to reach his or her IEP goal because all students have a different learning style and pace.

Evaluation Procedures

The evaluation procedure explains how and when the school nurse will assess progress on the student's IEP goal; it holds the nurse and the student accountable for reaching the annual IEP goal. Most school nurses will maintain frequent contact with students with IEPs they are providing nursing services to. It is important to always maintain and document record data on interfacing with the student or providing school nurse consultation on progress notes; paper notes may later be entered into a web-based special education program for documentation. When recording incidents involving maladaptive behavior, nurses should consider using an anecdotal behavior strategy that records the incident as well as behavior before and after the incident.

The evaluation procedure can take many forms: written reports, care logs, charts, conferences with the school nurse, observation logs, and others. The student's outcomes should be assessed regularly such as weekly or quarterly; the frequency depends on the specific goal and outcome. In an assessment of a student's outcome, language should reflect the student doing something such as "Student will demonstrate proper use of inhaler with spacer" or "Student will list the symptoms he or she will report to the nurse for management." One such outcome measure may be demonstrating something such as "Student will demonstrate to nurse accurate counting of carbs."

Schedule for Determining Student Progress

Maintaining sufficient data is key to determining proficiency on the IEP goal. Student progress toward and performance for each goal of his or her IEP will be reported at least as often as the school reports the performance of all students (per IDEA 2004 law). Nurses should indicate on the IEP form the schedule (daily, weekly, monthly, quarterly, or other) on which the student's progress on the IEP annual goal will be documented. If documentation is on a nurse's form such as a medication administration record, that information will also be documented on IEP forms on the schedule determined.

For example, the nurse documents daily that the student came without prompts to the nurse for medication; any necessary prompts should be noted as well. Special education teachers and other support staff will also write on the student's quarterly IEP report card or enter information into the student's computerized program about the student's progress or lack of it. Many IEP forms also include a section to document the dates the progress was reviewed.

Any Medicaid payments to the student's school should be documented to demonstrate the school nurse's services and accountability; this should follow state directives from the Medicaid agency about further requirements for proper billing procedures.

If the student is exceeding a goal or not making or maintaining progress toward a goal, the goal may need to be changed whenever the goal-setting components of the IEP are reevaluated.

Here are examples of language that can be used in the evaluation procedure and schedule for determining student's progress:

- Student will come to the school nurse's office for medication daily without prompting (benchmarks/short-term objectives)
    - 3/5 (evaluation criteria) times per week in the first marking quarter
    - 4/5 (evaluation criteria) times per week in the second marking quarter
    - 5/5 (evaluation criteria) times per week in the third marking quarter
- Student will come to the school nurse's office for medication daily without prompting (benchmarks/short-term objectives)
    - 80 percent (evaluation criteria) of the time per week in the first marking quarter
    - 90 percent (evaluation criteria) of the time per week in the second marking quarter
    - 100 percent (evaluation criteria) of the time per week in the third marking quarter
- Student will demonstrate learning about his or her asthma triggers (benchmarks/short-term objectives) by listing those asthma triggers
    - 3/5 (evaluation criteria) of known asthma triggers first marking quarter
    - 4/5 (evaluation criteria) of known asthma triggers second marking quarter
    - 5/5 (evaluation criteria) of known asthma triggers third marking quarter

Scaffolding Annual Goals and Objectives

The samples below illustrate what measurable annual goals and benchmarks might look like.

Measurable Annual Goals and Benchmarks/Short-Term Objectives and Evaluation

Annual measurable goal: Tom will come to the nurse's office daily for medication to improve his focus in the classroom in the school setting.

- Short-term objective 1: Tom will come to the nurse's office daily for medication without prompting 3 out of 5 times per week during the first quarter.
- Short-term objective 2: Tom will come to the nurse's office daily for medication without prompting 4 out of 5 times per week during the second quarter.
- Short-term objective 3: Tom will come to the nurse's office daily for medication without prompting 5 out of 5 times during the third quarter.

In designing the measurable annual goal(s), the school district must also determine when periodic progress reports will be provided to the parents.

- Schedule for reporting progress: there must be documentation of when periodic reports on the progress of the student will be provided to the parent(s). This may include the use of quarterly or other periodic reports issued at the same time as report cards.
- Report of progress: the school district informs the parents of when they will be informed of student progress toward the goal, or the annual report card may identify another means of reporting progress toward the goal.

Step Three: School Nursing Interventions to Help IEP Students Achieve Annual Goals

Because the student's health issues and needs are derived directly from the needs identified in the health evaluation and verified in the PLAAFP as impacting learning and able to be addressed by the school nurse or health services staff, the nurse designs interventions. When considering what interventions may be most effective, consider these questions:

- How does the child function daily in school? Why would the student see the school nurse daily, weekly, or monthly per semester to improve his or her learning?
- What supported services (school nursing services) would likely help the student make progress in school?

- What is the student's level of acuity? Does the student need continuous nursing services one on one with a nurse? Does the student need nursing follow-up for a chronic or acute medical condition? Is the service of an individual aide or paraprofessional needed to support the student in activities of daily living (ADL) skills?
- Is attendance an issue that the school nurse could work to improve?
- What is the current level of the student's understanding of his or her health condition? Can he or she name the medications and their effect and efficacy?
- What can the student reasonably accomplish by the end of the year to improve school performance?
- What are the student's needs beyond the expected needs of his or her nondisabled peers in the same grade and at the same age?
- Will the school nurse need to provide consultation services to other staff to help them understand the student's health issues that are impacting learning? (Consider adding nursing consultation services with the classroom teacher to understand how the student is doing in the classroom.)

After reviewing those questions and others, the nurse will write the plan for delivering the interventions most likely to improve the student's learning outcomes.

When determining the elements of the nurse's plan of nursing or health services to be provided, the interventions to be provided, and the student's goal outcomes to be measured, it is necessary to deliver services in ways that minimize disruption of the student's classroom instruction.

While making the plan for service delivery child-focused, it is a good idea to discuss the best times to provide the child with direct service. The teacher, case manager, and parents should be involved in this conversation. Is lunchtime a good time? Maybe socialization skills will be listed among IEP goals, and participating in lunch and recess might be necessary and therefore not the time for nursing interventions. Recess might not be a good time if an energetic student needs to release some energy. Other options may be natural transitions between classes or activities such as during lineup times or class breaks for water and toileting.

Classroom disruption is difficult for any student and especially for a student who may be easily distracted and lacking consistent focus. Nurses should try to establish the student's preference and work with it as well as the teacher's preference when possible. In general, nursing services are provided out of the view of other students and particularly out of the view of other staff who do not have a vested interest in the student. However, most of the time, the effort required to reduce out-of-seat time through pull-out service delivery is also a consideration. Must the student be pulled out of class to receive the nursing service? Can it be done as a push-in service in the student's normal environment? Push-in service can occur during less academically rigorous class periods, homeroom, or lunch or perhaps in the hallway to minimize interruption of learning; it could occur during a passing period. Some nurses and the students they are monitoring establish codes or signals between themselves to verify if for instance a student who uses an inhaler has done so and is feeling okay—a simple agreed-upon thumbs-up between the student in the classroom and the nurse in the doorway might suffice.

If among the student's medical regimen are any medications taken outside school, the school nurse may want to include services to help the student and parents monitor the effects of those medications on the student during the school day. A nurse could ask that a doctor prescribe medication to be taken during the school day so the nurse can monitor that.

While nurses usually handle nursing interventions, other staff members can do so if state regulations allow that; these could include oral feeding assistance or diapering. Some of those services are delivered directly to the student; these can include medication administration, tube feeding, teaching transitional self-care, and indirect services such as consulting with other staff regarding observations for attention deficit disorder (ADD) or observation or collaboration on any other health services or issues the nurse has identified.

When including medication administration or any specific nursing care as an IEP service, it is helpful to not name the medication or the name of the person who is to provide the service as both may change, and any changes to an IEP must be preceded by an IEP change meeting.

Transferring School Nurse Interventions to Units of Time

Since 1993, every school may submit claims to the state Medicaid department if the school district has a written contract to bill Medicaid for support services. This law applies to nursing services, occupational therapy (OT), physical therapy (PT), speech therapy, and other related services if the student is enrolled in Medicaid.

The billable nursing interventions are usually only those prescribed by an authorized medical prescriber and outlined in the student's IEP. Nursing minutes become financially relevant when the school is submitting claims for reimbursement from the student's Medicaid. The most common unit of service for billing purposes is fifteen-minute increments. Regardless of what other districts do, nurses should follow their state's Medicaid program rules and regulations regarding billing for services.

When calculating minutes, nurses should include the preparation and follow-up time involved, not just the minutes spent in directly providing the service. For example, a tube feeding may run fifteen minutes, but it may take an extra fifteen minutes before and after the feeding to assemble the equipment, inspect the skin, and perform follow-up care and charting.

School Nursing Matrix to Determine Minutes

The following is a summary for school nursing minutes when determining direct nursing services delivered to the student.

Mild. General health is stable, but health condition/disability requires minimal interruption of time in the classroom. Student will receive nursing minutes from fifteen minutes per day, month, or semester based on the needs of the student; e.g., medication daily or nursing follow-up for mild asthma per semester.

Moderate. May require interruption of classroom time. Student will receive fifteen to thirty minutes per day to help with conditions such as poor asthma control, uncontrolled diabetes, seizures, occasional suctioning, or catheterization daily.

Severe. Health status is medically complex and requires major classroom adaptations and placement in a more restrictive environment. Health status may be a permanent condition or temporary due to an acute condition. May require transport with licensed nurse. This would require 75 to 750 minutes per week based on the needs of the student.

Profound. Health status is medically complex and fragile requiring major accommodations and adaptations in the most restrictive environment. Instability requires frequent interruptions, and transport requires a nurse. This designation would require 750 to 1,500 minutes per week for example for a medically fragile child with daily one-on-one nursing needs.

A medically fragile child is one whose complex medical conditions require professional nursing monitoring and supervision twenty-four hours a day to prevent life-threatening complications and deterioration of health status and to maintain health status.

Some nurses wonder what kind of student's health IEP goals they can write about the medically fragile students, those who need palliative care, or students with an end-of-life order such as DNR (Do Not Resuscitate), DNAR (Do Not Attempt Resuscitation), POLST (Physician Order for Life Sustaining Treatment), or MOST (Medical Orders for Scope of Treatment) or even if there should be IEP goals for such students. Those health IEP goals can and should be written even or perhaps especially because the student is medically fragile.

Here is an example of annual IEP health goals written for a medically fragile and nonverbal student receiving school nursing services:

PLAAFP: Jane is an eight-year-old female student who is medically fragile, in a wheelchair, nonverbal due to traumatic brain injury (TBI), requires daily gastrostomy tube (G-tube) feeding for forty-five minutes per day to maintain daily caloric intake.

Student's annual IEP goals:

Annual goal 1: Jane will turn her head when her name is called to acknowledge implementation of an activity about to occur (benchmark/short-term objective) such as tube feeding.

- 3/5 (evaluation criteria) times per week in the first marking quarter
- 4/5 (evaluation criteria) times per week in the second marking quarter
- 5/5 (evaluation criteria) times per week in the third marking quarter

Annual goal 2: Jane will assist in her G-tube feeding by maintaining clothing away from feeding site during the feeding (benchmark/short-term objective).

- 3/5 (evaluation criteria) times per week in the first marking quarter
- 4/5 (evaluation criteria) times per week in the second marking quarter
- 5/5 (evaluation criteria) times per week in the third marking quarter

Annual goal 3: Jane will position herself upright in her wheelchair (benchmark/short-term objective) to facilitate the flow of the food within the tubing.

- 3/5 (evaluation criteria) times per week in the first marking quarter
- 4/5 (evaluation criteria) times per week in the second marking quarter
- 5/5 (evaluation criteria) times per week in the third marking quarter

Nurses should review the student's health IEP goal at least once a month for a young student and every two to three months for an older one. It is important for nurses to discuss with older students how the support services (school nursing) are helping them achieve academic success. It would be important to discuss with a student with asthma how better asthma management has allowed him or her to improve school attendance, stay in the classroom more, and not miss classroom instruction or after-school activities.

How Is the Student's IEP Progress Measured Annually?

A federal requirement is that the IEP be reviewed at least annually to discuss the student's progress within the IEP. Those conducting the review must include those who were involved in the original case study evaluation (CSE) or IEP meeting or their equivalently credentialed replacements. The school nurse may attend and discuss how the student with a health condition may be following his or her medication regimen by coming regularly without prompting to the nurse for medication. This observation may be particularly useful regarding a student with attention deficit disorder (ADD) or attention deficit hyperactivity disorder (ADHD) who is coming regularly to the nurse for medication. The teacher may state at the annual IEP meeting that the student's work is improving and she or he is focusing better in the classroom. This combined data is important to understand the value of the student coming for daily medication to improve learning.

Sometimes, it can take more than a year to see significant progress in the area of some of the needs of the children, or the IEP team including parents may discover that the goals as written are unattainable or met very easily. The IEP team may with proper notice reconvene to rewrite the goals and/or benchmarks.

CHAPTER 7

Sample IEP Goals as Written by School Nurse

Sample IEP goal, student with ADHD						
IDEA eligibility category that meets criteria for eligibility for IEP	Nursing diagnosis using NANDA definition	Student goal related to health (from PLAAFP)	Student goal related to academics from PLAAFP. May be helpful to refer to the academic goals of other IEP team members	Nursing intervention	Desired student outcome/ goal and evaluation measurement written in short steps with measurements that are measurable, achievable, time-defined, i.e., benchmarks across a school year that increase, decrease, or maintain the achievement or frequency of the measurement.	Outcomes (progress) at least annually according to the written time frame, e.g. quarterly, twice a year, annually. *May be reported on student's report card as well.

OHI: having limited strength, vitality, or alertness including a heightened alertness to environmental stimuli that results in limited alertness with respect to the educational environment due to a chronic or acute health problem that adversely affects a child's educational performance.	Altered sensory perception	Decreased response to external stimuli not related to educational activity	Increase time on task	If medication prescribed: administer medication, assess response; communicate with parents and prescriber as needed. Additionally or if not on medication: consult with family on evidence-based behavioral methods to treat inattentiveness	Student will increase time on task from baseline of 50% of a 20-minute lesson as measured quarterly by observation and time-on-task measurements	Student will increase time on task from baseline 50% of a 20-minute lesson to 75% then to 90% as measured annually over the course of the three-year plan
	Add additional nursing diagnoses where relevant					

*Reminder: Whether solely health related or academics related, the goals written in the IEP refer to the concerns identified in the domain meeting related to health and related to the disability category. The goals reference the unique needs of the student's health-related concerns written in the PLAAFP, are student centered, and address what the student needs to make progress in his specialized instruction.

Sample IEP goal for student with multiple disabilities: eight-year-old female student is quadriplegic and nonverbal with limited self-awareness and dependent on feedings by G-tube.

IDEA eligibility category that meets criteria for eligibility for IEP	Nursing diagnosis using NANDA definition	Student Goal related to health (from PLAAFP)	Student goal related to academics (from PLAAFP) May be helpful to refer to the academic goals of other IEP team members	Nursing Intervention	Desired Student outcome/goal and evaluation measurement written in short steps with measurements that are measurable, achievable, time-defined, i.e. benchmarks across a school year that increase, decrease, or maintain the achievement or frequency of measurement	Outcomes (progress) at least annually but completed according to the written time frame, e.g. quarterly, twice a year, annually. *May be reported on student's report card as well.
Multiple disabilities	Feeding self-care deficit	Maintain adequate nutrition for daily activities and growth	Student will not be distracted by hunger or gastric complaints detrimental to academic interventions	Provide proper G-tube feeding on schedule per HCP orders; maintain stoma skin integrity	Will demonstrate satiety and/or lack of hunger by attending to teaching staff, demonstrated by eye contact, tracking, and other methods observed by teaching staff	By end of 3 year term of this IEP, will demonstrate adequate nutrition and skin integrity by lab reports and medical progress notes

	Altered response to stimuli	Increase interaction with staff to communicate needs	Increase interaction with staff to increase communication abilities	Self-awareness of surroundings and staff interventions	Will turn her head when her name is called 3 out of 5 times; then 4 of 5 then 5 of 5 yearly, measured quarterly	By end of 3-year term of IEP, will demonstrate responsiveness by turning head 5/5 times upon hearing name
*Reminder: Whether solely health related or academics related, the goals written in the IEP refer to the concerns identified in the domain meeting related to health and related to the disability category. The goals reference the unique needs of the student's health-related concerns written in the PLAAFP, are student centered, and address what the student needs to make progress in his specialized instruction.						

Extended School Year Services

If students qualify for year-round or extended school year (ESY) services, they can continue beyond the school year in accordance with the child's IEP at no cost to the parents. If that is the case, nurses should address how the nursing or health services will be provided during that extension. Will the district hire a nursing agency? If so, who will orient agency staff to that student's health needs?

CHAPTER 8

Writing Other Student Health Care Plans

Most state Nurse Practice Acts include within the RN's scope of work the responsibility to develop a care plan. In addition to writing the IEP and the student's health goals, school nurses also write other health care plans not necessarily related to the student's IEP. For a student with an IEP, these other plans may be part of the IEP or be referred to in the IEP. For example, for a student with a specific learning disability (SLD) who also has asthma that has not been determined to affect the student's learning, a nurse may write an individual health care plan (IHCP) or an emergency care plan (ECP; also called an emergency action plan, EAP) to address the student's asthma issues. An IHCP or ECP or other care plans may be written into the IEP program for students with IEPs whose health issues are determined to be directly related to the learning disability (LD).

Points to Consider about Health Care Plans for Students with IEPs or Other Students with Medical Conditions

- Write an individual health care plan (IHCP) detailing the health-related interventions that will be provided in school for the student and distribute to the teacher(s) to follow; these can include students with asthma, diabetes, or any other major health problems that are adversely affecting the student's learning.
- Write an ECP or EAP if indicated for students with life-threatening medical issues such as asthma, diabetes, cardiac problems, history of anaphylaxis, and other conditions.
- Follow all state requirements related to the provision of medications to students and related to the provision of nursing services, including whether delegating nursing services to non-health care licensed personnel is acceptable or prohibited.
- Follow your state laws and regulations for writing your IHCP or ECP.
- Contact your school nurse manager or state consultants for any questions regarding the care and safety for the students in your school.

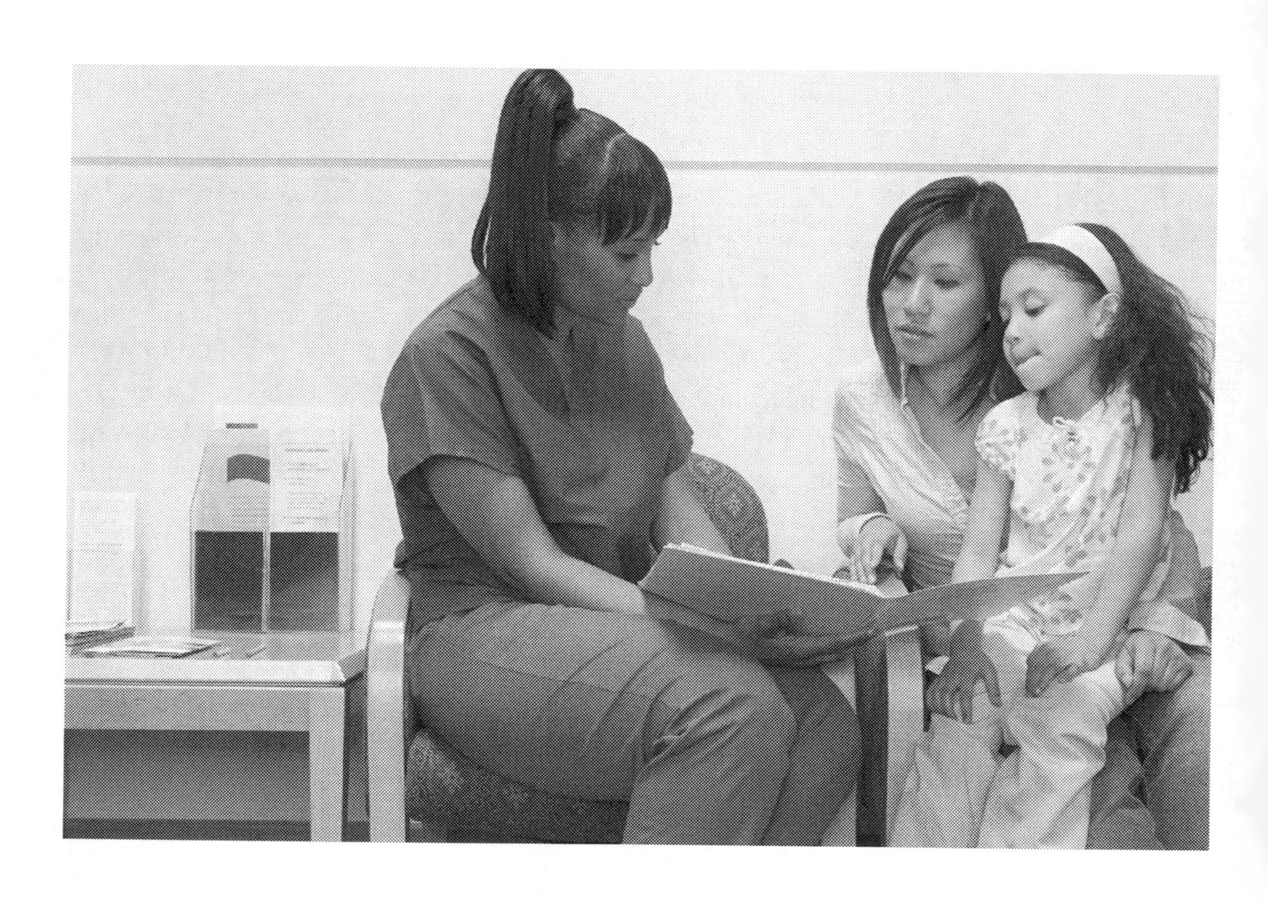

CONCLUSION

We wrote this book to support school nurses who assist in developing and implementing special education programs from our perspectives as experienced school nurses, school nurse educators, and school nurse consultants. We wrote it for novice school nurses and more-experienced school nurses who want to review best practices and guidance on performing more-focused student health evaluations and outcomes.

School nurses can refer to their own state school nurse consultants (www.schoolnurseconsultants.org) and their state and local education agencies for further specific guidance related to policies and rules in their work locations.

This book is also a resource for administrators, directors, and others in school special education departments to inform them of the role of the school nurse in developing student-specific IEPs.

We hope readers will use this book to learn more about special education, to review a student's health for its effect on academics, and to fully incorporate the student with special needs into school life.

As former practicing school nurses, we commend all the school nurses across this country for their dedicated work on behalf of students whether disabled or not to achieve success in their health and academics.

> Let us never consider ourselves finished nurses … We must be learning all of our lives.
> —Florence Nightingale; accessed March 29, 2019, a-z quotes

GLOSSARY

This glossary provides definitions of terms often used in special education with a multidisciplinary perspective. Content is partially adapted from https://www.understandingspecialeducation.com/special-education-terms.html, with permission, revised for relevance to school nurses.

ABC analysis. One of the educational strategies for analyzing student behavior; a systematic recording of antecedents, behaviors, and consequences as a strategy for analyzing student behavior.

absence seizure. Seizure that is brief and often characterized by momentary lapses of attention. Also called a petit mal seizure.

accommodations. Changes that allow a student with a disability to participate fully in an activity. Examples include extended time, different test formats, and alterations to a classroom.

adapted physical education (APE). Specially designed physical education program using accommodations designed to fit the needs of students who require developmental or corrective instruction in PE.

adaptive behavior. The collection of conceptual, social, and practical skills people have learned so they can function in their everyday lives.

ADD/ADHD. See *attention deficit disorder* and *attention deficit hyperactivity disorder.*

administrator. Professional responsible for managing some aspect of schools: includes principals, assistant principals, department chair, team leaders, special coordinators, district administrators, and others.

advance organizer. A teaching method that presents information as organizational signals that make content more understandable by putting it in a more general framework. See other types of organizer teaching methods defined in this glossary.

adverse effect. See *impact statement.*

advocate. Individual who works to ensure that parents understand their rights and that school professionals provide a plan agreeable to the parents.

alternative test site. A change in where a student with a disability is tested to make sure the results of the test are valid. An example is testing a student with attention problems in a room having fewer distractions.

alternative ways of administering tests. Testing adaptations that involve changing the ways students respond on tests and/or ways teachers give tests. An example of changing the way students respond on tests is by having them do so orally. An example of changing the way teachers give tests is giving a test orally.

Americans with Disabilities Act (ADA). Civil rights law passed in 1990 that protects individuals with disabilities from discrimination and requires building and transportation accessibility and reasonable accommodations in the workplace.

Americans with Disabilities Act Amendment Act (ADAAA). Civil rights law passed in 2008 that revised the original 1990 ADA.

anecdotal record, anecdotal recording. Strategy and procedure for recording and analyzing objective, narrative descriptions of the observations of a student's behavior in which incidents before and after a behavior are recorded along with a description of the behavior.

annual goal. Broad statement describing estimated yearly outcomes for a student with a disability; annual goals address areas of identified needs.

annual IEP meeting. See *annual review.*

annual review. The IEP team will convene at least annually to discuss the student's progress in the IEP. Those conducting the review include a parent, teacher, administrator, and others as needed to review and update a student's IEP.

anxiety. Condition in which an individual experiences extraordinary worry in some situations or worries excessively about future situations. In children, anxiety is commonly accompanied by extreme agitation filled with tension and dread. Anxiety is different from fear. Children with anxiety may or may not qualify for special education. Those who need modifications to their school day may be able to achieve reduced anxiety through a Section 504 plan.

Asperger's syndrome. A term previously used to describe a syndrome related to autism in which the individual with the syndrome may be intellectually gifted rather than intellectually disabled but possesses other symptoms of autism. The term is no longer a diagnosis on its own as it is now part of a broader category of autism now known as autism spectrum disorder.

assessment. As the first step in the nursing process, the collecting of information about a student to help make decisions about the student's program of instruction. May also refer to the entire testing and diagnostic processes leading up to the development of an appropriate IEP for a student with special education needs. see evaluation

assessment planning. A format or process sometimes dictated by a state education department or school district to describe the evaluation of issues involving health conditions.

assistive technology (AT). Any of a wide variety of technology applications designed to help students with disabilities to learn, communicate, and otherwise function more independently by bypassing their disabilities.

at risk. Having a high potential for experiencing future medical or learning problems.

attachment disorder. A psychiatric illness that can develop in young children as early as their first birthday that causes problems with emotional attachments to others. The cause may be unknown or may be in conjunction with homelessness, parental abandonment, parental emotional disorders, and so forth. Sometimes related to autism spectrum disorder.

attention deficit disorder (ADD), attention deficit hyperactivity disorder (ADHD). A psychiatric medical condition characterized by a child's inability to focus while possessing impulsivity, fidgeting, inattention, distractibility, and/or hyperactivity.

auditory processing disorder (APD). Also known as a central auditory processing disorder, this condition adversely affects how sound is processed or interpreted by the brain. Individuals with APD do not recognize subtle differences between sounds in words even when the sounds are loud and clear enough to be heard and may find it difficult to tell where sounds are coming from, to make sense of the order of sounds, or to block out competing background noises.

authentic assessment. A performance-based assessment technique of the student's application of knowledge to real-life activities, real-world settings, or a simulation of such settings using real-life, real-world activities.

autism. A brain development disorder characterized by impaired social interaction including communication with onset in early childhood and not known to be caused by any other behavioral or medical condition.

autism spectrum disorder. Contemporary term used to convey the diversity of autism and related disorders.

baseline measure. The level or frequency of behavior prior to the implementation of an instructional procedure that is later evaluated.

basic skills instruction. Instruction in the tool skills of reading, writing, and math.

behavior contract. Agreement between a teacher or other adult and student that clearly specifies student performance expectations, rewards for meeting expectations, consequences of not meeting expectations, and the time for which the agreement is valid.

behavior intervention plan (BIP). Special education term used to describe the written plan used to address problem behavior that includes positive behavioral interventions, strategies, and support.

benchmark. A standard or point of reference against which things may be compared or assessed. It sets the start or point of reference by which progress within the IEP may be measured.

bipolar disorder. Characterized by cycles of mania alternating with depression. Children with bipolar disorder go through unusual mood changes; because of the familiar mood changes that often accompany adolescence, school nurses should be aware of normal mood changes vs. extreme and disabling mood changes.

blindness. Condition defined by lacking visual perception due to physiological or neurological factors. A student who qualifies under this disability may have some sight, but the sight is limited in usefulness to a marked degree.

Braille. Writing system used by individuals who have vision impairments that uses various combinations of six raised dots punched on paper and read or decoded with the fingertips.

brainstorming. Strategy for generating solutions to problems in which participants call out ideas and building on one another's responses while deferring all evaluation.

case study evaluation (CSE). A full evaluation including all its components to study and analyze the child's abilities as well as skills to link the cause and the result of any identified disabilities if possible.

central auditory processing disorder, See auditory processing disorder (APD)"

certified school nurse (CSN). A credential applied to a nurse who has met national or state requirement to obtain a certificate in this specialty. The credential standardizes the profession and is a way to measure a school nurse candidate's additional knowledge and experience. Contact each state's school nurse consultant (www.schoolnurseconsultants.org) for more information on state certification; information on national certification is available through the National Board for Certification of School Nurses (www.nbcsn.org).

child abuse. Situation in which a parent or other caregiver inflicts or allows others to inflict injury on a child or permits a substantial risk of injury to exist. In some states, all school staff, not only school nurses, must take a course on child abuse and neglect and report suspected abuse or neglect.

child neglect. Situation in which a parent or other caregiver fails to provide the necessary supports for a child's well-being. In some states, all school staff, not only school nurses, must take a course on child abuse and neglect and report suspected abuse or neglect.

classroom organization. Strategies through which a teacher establishes and maintains order in a classroom.

cognitive behavior management. Behavior management strategy in which students learn to monitor and change their own behavior.

complaint procedure. A formal document initiated by a parent or child advocate filed with the district, county, or state board of education alleging that the school or district may have violated requirements of the Individuals with Disabilities Education Act (IDEA) or a local policy or procedure.

consultant. Specialist who provides expertise to teachers and others when an extraordinary student need arises.

consulting teacher. Special education teacher who meets with general education teachers to problem solve and monitor student progress but who typically has little or no direct contact with students.

cooperative learning. Student-centered instructional approach in which students work in small, mixed-ability groups with a shared learning goal.

coteaching. Instructional approach in which two or more teachers or other certified staff share instruction for a single group of students in a single classroom setting. Also referred to as *parallel teaching* and *team teaching*.

cross-categorical approach. Instructional approach in which the cognitive, learning, affective, and social and emotional needs of students, not their disability labels, form the basis for planning and delivering instruction.

cue words. Words that make patterns of information more conspicuous for students such as the words *similar* and *different* that signal the presence of a compare/contrast pattern.

cumulative file. The records maintained by the local school district for any child enrolled in school. The file may contain evaluation and information about a child's disability and placement. It also contains grades and the results of standardized assessments. Parents have the right to inspect these files at any time.

curriculum-based assessment (CBA). A direct evaluation of skills that form part of the test-takers' curriculum. The test of performance in this case comes directly from the curriculum. Method of measuring the level of achievement of students in terms of what they are taught in the classroom.

curriculum-based measurement. A kind of curriculum-based assessment (CBA) characterized by a research base establishing its technical adequacy as well as standardized measurement tasks that are fluency based.

daily activity log. Strategy for providing ongoing information for students and their parents about learning by noting daily observations of student work, effort, and outcomes.

deaf-blindness. Means concomitant hearing and visual impairments, the combination of which causes such severe communication and other developmental and educational needs that they cannot be accommodated in special education programs solely for children with deafness or children with blindness.

deafness. Hearing impairment that is so severe that a child is impaired in possessing any linguistic information through hearing with or without amplification that adversely affects his or her educational performance.

decibel (dB). Unit for measuring the loudness of sounds.

decoding. Reading skill involving accurately identifying words and pronouncing them fluently.

degree of accuracy. The extent to which a student's academic performance is without errors.

depression. Condition in which an individual is persistently and seriously unhappy with a loss of interest or pleasure in all or almost all usual activities. Symptoms of depression include changes in appetite or weight, sleep disturbances, loss of energy, feelings of worthlessness, and thoughts of death or suicide.

designated instruction services (DIS). Instruction and services not normally provided by regular classes, resource specialist programs (RSPs), or special day classes. They include speech therapy and adaptive physical education.

developmental delay (DD). Significant delay in physical, cognitive, communication, social or emotional, or adaptive development, or a combination in children ages three to nine or any subset of that range.
The IDEA permits the use of this term in lieu of a more specific disability label for children until age nine.

diagnosis. In education, a type of assessment decision concerning whether a student meets established federal guidelines for being classified as having a disability and if so the nature and extent of the disability.

diagnostic teaching. Sample lessons and other instructional activities carried out with students experiencing extreme academic or behavioral difficulty as part of screening.

differentiated instruction. A form of instruction that meets students' diverse needs by providing materials and tasks of varied levels of difficulty with varying degrees of support through multiple instructional groups and time variations.

direct instruction. Research-based instructional approach in which the teacher presents subject matter using a review of previously taught information, presentation of new concepts or skills, guided practice, feedback, correction, independent student practice, and frequent review.

disability. According to the Americans with Disabilities Act, a physical or mental impairment that substantially limits one or more major life activities. In education, it also refers to difficulty so severe that it negatively affects student learning.

discipline. Term to describe the set of classroom expectations including rules for behavior that serve as a means for facilitating student learning.

DNR (Do Not Resuscitate): end-of-life orders or orders for levels of treatment for persons receiving palliative care. Similar terms are DNAR (Do Not Attempt Resuscitation), POLST (Physician Order for Life Sustaining Treatment) and MOST (Medical Orders for Scope of Treatment).

domain meeting. A formal meeting to address the different students' domain areas or sections in the assessment process. Domain sections to address are: academic achievement, functional performance, cognitive function, communication status, health, hearing and vision, motor ability, and social/emotional conditions

due process. In education, steps and processes outlined in law that protect the rights of students with disabilities including the right of a parent to disagree with a school district's special education program recommendations. May be preceded by another option to resolve such as dispute, mediation.

dyscalculia. A specific learning disability (SLD) that affects a person's ability to understand numbers and learn math facts. Those with this type of learning disability may also have poor comprehension of math symbols, may struggle with memorizing and organizing numbers, have difficulty telling time, or have trouble with counting.

dysgraphia. A specific learning disability (SLD) that affects a person's handwriting ability and fine motor skills. Problems may include illegible handwriting, inconsistent spacing, poor spatial planning on paper, poor spelling, and difficulty composing writing as well as thinking and writing at the same time.

dyslexia. A specific learning disability (SLD) that affects reading and related language-based processing skills. The severity can differ in each individual but can affect reading fluency, decoding, reading comprehension, recall, writing, spelling, and sometimes speech; it can exist along with other related disorders. Dyslexia is sometimes referred to as a language-based learning disability.

early intervention services (EIS). Programs that provide support and services for families of children through thirty-five months of age who are exhibiting developmental delay (DD) in meeting developmental milestones.

Education for All Handicapped Children Act (EHCA). See *Public Law 94-124*.

eligibility determination conference (EDC). The meeting at which all parties provide evaluation reports and come to a conclusion as to whether or not the child or student meets conditions for eligibility for special education services per definitions proscribed in IDEA 2004 and federal US Department of Education regulations.

emergency action plan (EAP), emergency care plan (ECP). A plan usually written by the school nurse to assist all school staff in providing care to a child known to have a life-threatening health condition.

emotional disturbance (ED). Term used to describe a diagnosable mental, behavioral, or emotional disorder that lasts for a significant duration that meets the criteria within the *Diagnostic and Statistical Manual of Mental Disorders*. Condition in which an individual has significant difficulty in the social and emotional domain so much so that it interferes with learning.

English-language learners (ELLs). Student whose native language is not English and who is developing English-language skills in school.

enrichment. Approach for educating gifted and talented students based on helping them elaborate on or extend concepts being presented to all students.

evaluation. Procedures used to determine whether teaching is effective to provide feedback to students and their parents about student learning and to inform school boards and communities about school effectiveness. In nursing, evaluation is the procedure by which the nursing interventions are determined effective to improve student health.

Every Student Succeeds Act (ESSA). Federal law enacted in 2015 that governs K–12 public education. Replaced No Child Left Behind Act.

evidence-based practice (EBP). Instructional techniques and nursing interventions that have been shown by research to be most likely to improve student outcomes in a meaningful way.

example selection. Teacher choice of examples during instruction. Example selection directly affects student understanding of instruction.

executive function, executive functioning (EF). The cognitive management systems of the brain that affects a variety of skills in neuropsychological processes such as planning, organization, strategizing, paying attention to and remembering details, managing time and space, emotional regulation control, task initiative, transition between tasks, impulse control, and self-monitoring. Different patterns of weakness in executive functioning are almost always seen in the learning profiles of those with specific learning disabilities or attention deficit hyperactivity disorder (ADHD).

expressive language. An individual's ability to communicate meaning clearly through speech.

extended school year services (ESY). An extended school year is a component of special education services for students with unique needs who require services that go beyond the regular academic year. Extended year often refers to summer school.

free appropriate public education (FAPE). An educational right of disabled children guaranteed by the Rehabilitation Act of 1973 and the Individuals with Disabilities Education Act (IDEA); https://www2.ed.gov/about/offices/list/ocr/docs/edlite-FAPE504.html.

Family Educational Rights and Privacy Act (FERPA). Federal law that protects the privacy of student education records. The law applies to all schools that receive funds under an applicable program of the US Department of Education. https://www2.ed.gov/policy/gen/guid/fpco/ferpa/index.html; (20 U.S.C. § 1232g; 34 CFR Part 99).

functional behavior assessment. The process of gathering detailed data on a student's behavior and the context in which it occurs for the purpose of determining the reasons for it and creating a behavior intervention plan (BIP). This process is required by federal law when a student with a disability has significant behavior problems.

general education teacher. Elementary, middle school, junior high, or high school teacher whose primary responsibility is teaching one or more groups of classes to students who are generally normally developing.

grade equivalent (GE). A measure of the score that would be achieved by students in the stated grade on the same instrument. For example, a GE of 6.2 identifies a score that would be achieved by students in the second month of grade six taking the same test. A very general score.

grading contract. Agreement between a teacher and student that specifies the quantity, quality, and timeliness of work required to receive a specific grade.

grading criteria. The standard by which a student's academic performance is evaluated and graded.

graphic organizer. Visual format that helps students organize their understanding of information being presented or read and the relationships between various parts of the information.

group administered standardized achievement test. Standardized achievement test given to large groups of students at one time usually administered by general education teachers; useful as a screening measure.

hard of hearing. Hearing impairment in which an individual has some hearing through which to process linguistic information possibly with the assistance of hearing aids or other assistive devices.

hearing impairment. Condition in which an individual has the inability or limited ability to receive information auditorily such that it interferes with learning. Full or partial decrease in the ability to detect or understand sounds.

hertz. A measure of pitch in a hearing screening or hearing evaluation.

high-incidence disability. Any of the more frequently occurring disabilities encountered in classrooms among the disabilities outlined in IDEA including communication disorders, intellectual disabilities, specific learning disabilities, emotional or behavioral disorders, and physical and sensory needs.

home/hospital instruction. Students with verified medical conditions that prevent them from attending school may receive services temporarily in the home or hospital with a physician's referral.

homework. The most common form of student practice.

hyperactive-impulsive disorder. Type of attention deficit hyperactivity disorder (ADHD) characterized by excessive movement and other motor activity including fidgeting, a need to move around a room even when others are seated, and rapid changes in activities.

impact statement. A statement of the extent to which an evaluation measure or disability is believed to be impacting or adversely affecting the educational progress or school performance of the student to a level below those of similar age peers.

impulsivity. Non-goal-oriented activity exhibited by individuals who lack careful thought and reflection prior to behavior. The extent to which an individual acts before thinking; often a characteristic of students with high-incidence disabilities or attention deficit hyperactivity disorder (ADHD)

inclusion. Term used to describe services that place students with disabilities in general education classrooms with appropriate support services. Student may receive instruction from both a general education teacher and a special education teacher.

independent educational evaluation (IEE). The right of a parent to request an evaluation conducted by a qualified examiner who is not employed by the school district in addition to the school or district's evaluation. The school district pays for the evaluation unless the school or district challenges the request, in which case the parent may file a complaint or obtain an evaluation at their own expense and enter due-process protection for reimbursement.

independent learning skills. Skills students need to manage their school learning including note taking, textbook reading, test taking, written expression, and time management.

indirect instruction. A type of teaching based on the belief that children are naturally active learners and that given the appropriate instructional environment, they will actively construct knowledge and solve problems in developmentally appropriate ways.

individual health care plan (IHCP or IHP). Documents written by the nurse or other health professional detailing the health-related interventions that will be provided in school.

individualized education program (IEP). A written educational program that outlines the current levels of performance, related services, educational goals, and modifications for a student with a disability. This plan is developed by a team including the student's parent(s), teacher(s), and support staff. Document prepared by the multidisciplinary team or annual review team that specifies a student's level of functioning and needs, the instructional goals and objectives for the student and how they will be evaluated, the nature and extent of special education and related services to be received, and the initiation date and duration of the services.

individualized education program team, multidisciplinary team, interdisciplinary team. The collective efforts of individuals from a variety of disciplines in assessing the needs of a student. Team including teachers, specialists, administrators, and parents who assess a student's individual needs, determine eligibility for special education, and develop the IEP. The committee may also include medical professional and other relevant parties.

individualized family service plan (IFSP). Education plan for children receiving services through P.L. 99-457; similar to an IEP. A process of providing early intervention services for children up to age three with special needs. Family-based needs are identified, and a written plan is developed and reviewed periodically.

individualized grading. Accommodations made for individual students that are included in their IEPs. Individualized grading includes accommodations that involve changing the elements being graded such as curriculum content, class participation, and homework or the value or weights assigned these elements.

individualized instruction. Instruction designed to meet the specific needs of a student with a disability; a requirement of IDEA.

individualized transition plan (ITP), transition IEP. The IEP of an adolescent must include by age sixteen plans to addresses areas of postschool activities, postsecondary education, employment, community experiences, and daily living skills and the services needed to achieve these goals.

Individuals with Disabilities Education Act (IDEA). Federal law that updates the 1975 Education for All Handicapped Children Act; original legislation guaranteeing students with disabilities a free and appropriate public education and the right to be educated with their nondisabled peers. The most recent revision occurred in 2004.

informal tests. Assessment techniques that are not intended to provide a comparison with a broader group beyond the students in the local project.

instructional accommodations. Services or supports provided to help students gain full access to class content and instruction, and help them accurately demonstrate what they know.

instructional assistance team. Team of teachers, specialists, and administrators that solves problems for students experiencing academic or behavioral difficulties and decides whether students should be individually assessed for possible special education services.

interdisciplinary team. See individualized education program team."

intervention. Preventive, remedial, compensatory, or survival services made on behalf of an individual with a disability.

instructional modifications. Changes in classroom instruction that involve altering student content expectations and performance outcomes.

integration. The physical, social, and instructional assimilation of students with disabilities into general education settings.

intellectual disability. Significantly below-average general intellectual functioning existing concurrently with deficits in adaptive behavior and manifested during the developmental period that adversely affects a child's educational performance. Term sometimes used as a synonym for *mental retardation.*

itinerant teacher. Special education teacher or service provider who provides services to students with disabilities and teaches in more than one school or district.

language processing disorder (LPD). A specific type of auditory processing disorder (APD) in which there is difficulty attaching meaning to sound groups that form words, sentences, and stories. While an APD affects the interpretation of all sounds coming into the brain, an LPD relates only to the processing of language. An LPD can affect expressive language and/or receptive language.

learning disability (LD). Condition in which a student has dysfunction in processing information typically found in language-based activities that interferes with learning. Students with LDs have at least average intelligence but experience significant problems in learning how to read, write, and/or do math.

learning outcomes. Specific goals or outcomes students are expected to accomplish as a result of a unit of instruction.

learning strategies. Techniques, principles, or rules that enable a student to solve problems and complete tasks independently.

least restrictive environment (LRE). An educational setting for exceptional students and students with disabilities that minimizes their exclusion from students without disabilities. The placement of students with special needs in a manner promoting the maximum possible interaction with the general school population. Placement options are offered on a continuum including regular classroom with no support services, regular classroom with support services, designated instruction services (DIS), special day classes, and private special education programs.

lesson organizer routine. A teaching method that helps teachers convert content into understandable formats that meet the diverse needs of students. The method has three components: the lesson organizer device, linking steps, and cue-do-review sequence.

local education agency. Term used to describe a school district; also called local education authority.

low-incidence disability. Any of the less common disabilities outlined in IDEA including multiple disabilities, hearing impairments, orthopedic impairments, other health impairments, visual impairments, deaf-blindness, autism, and traumatic brain injury (TBI).

mainstreaming. Also defined as "inclusion"; used to describe the integration of children with special needs into general education classrooms for part of the school day when they can meet traditional academic expectations with minimal assistance or when those expectations are not relevant. The remainder of the day, if relevant, is in a special education classroom.

manifestation determination. Within ten school days of any decision to change the placement of a child with a disability because of violation of school rule or code of conduct, the IEP team must review all relevant information in the student's file to determine if the conduct in question was caused by the child's disability or if the conduct was a direct result of the school district's failure to implement the child's IEP.

manipulatives. Concrete objects or representational items used as part of instruction. Examples of commonly used manipulatives include blocks and counters.

mediation. Process in which a neutral professional assists parents and school district personnel in resolving disputes concerning any aspect of a student's special education.

medically fragile child. A child whose complex medical conditions require professional nursing monitoring and supervision on a twenty-four-hour basis to prevent life-threatening complications, prevent deterioration of health status, and/or to maintain health status.

mobility specialist. Specialist who helps students with visual impairments learn to become familiar with their environments and able to travel from place to place independently and safely.

model. Concrete representation that can help students make connections between abstractions and real-life physical objects or processes.

multidisciplinary team. See individualized education program team."

multiple disabilities. An IEP term used to define a combination of disabilities that causes severe educational needs that require multiple special education programs such as mental retardation with blindness, the combination of which causes severe educational needs that cannot be accommodated in special education programs solely for one of the impairments. Multiple disabilities do not include deaf-blindness.

multisensory approach. Instructional approach that emphasizes the use of more than one modality for teaching and learning. For example, having a student read a vocabulary word, spell it aloud, and write it is a multisensory approach to teaching vocabulary.

native language. The primary language used by an individual.

No Child Left Behind Act of 2001. Reauthorization of the Elementary and Secondary Education Act of 1965; this law set high standards for student achievement and increased accountability for student learning. Replaced by Every Student Succeeds Act (ESSA).

nonpublic school. Districts contract with special education focused on nonpublic schools when an appropriate placement cannot be found in the scope of the public education setting. Nonpublic school placement is sought only after efforts to find appropriate placement in public schools have been exhausted. Also known as therapeutic day school, therapeutic boarding school, residential placement school.

nonverbal learning disability (NVD or NVLD). A disorder characterized usually by a significant discrepancy between higher verbal skills and weaker motor, visual-spatial, and social skills. Typically, an individual with NLD or NVLD has trouble interpreting nonverbal cues such as facial expressions or body language and may have poor coordination.

nursing diagnosis. May be a part of the nursing process and is a clinical judgment about individual, family, or community experiences and responses to actual or potential health problems or life processes.

nursing services. Services that may be provided only by a registered nurse, licensed practical nurse, or licensed vocational nurse according to each state's laws on nursing scope of practice.

obsessive-compulsive disorder (OCD). OCD is an anxiety disorder that presents itself as recurrent and persistent obsessions or compulsions. Obsessions are intrusive ideas, thoughts, or images while compulsions are repetitive behaviors or mental acts a child feels he or she must perform.

occupational therapist, occupational therapy (OT). Specialist with expertise in meeting students' needs in the area of fine motor skills including self-help skills such as feeding and dressing. Consults with and provides support to staff to improve a student's educational performance related to fine motor, gross motor, and sensory integration development.

one-on-one instruction. Classroom grouping arrangement in which individual students work with either a teacher or on computer in materials geared to their level and at their own pace.

oppositional defiant disorder (ODD). A child who defies authority by disobeying, talking back, arguing, or being hostile excessively compared to other children for more than six months. May also occur with other behavioral problems such as attention deficit hyperactivity disorder (ADHD), learning disabilities, and anxiety disorders.

orthopedic impairment. Term used to define skeletal impairments caused by congenital anomalies, impairments by diseases (e.g., poliomyelitis, bone tuberculosis, bone cancer) and impairments from other causes (e.g., cerebral palsy, amputations due to disease or injury, and fractures or burns that cause contractures) that seriously impair a student's ability to move about or to complete motor activities and interfere with learning.

other health impairment. Term used to describe limited strength, vitality, and alertness including a heightened alertness to environment stimuli that results in limited ability in the educational environment. Impairment could be a result of chronic health problems such as asthma, attention deficit disorder (ADD), diabetes, epilepsy, heart conditions, hemophilia, lead poisoning, leukemia, nephritis, rheumatic fever, sickle cell anemia, and Tourette's syndrome and adversely affects a child's educational performance.

outcome-based assessment. The evaluation of skills that are important in real life.

paraprofessional. Unlicensed or uncertified staff member employed to assist licensed or certified staff in carrying out education programs and otherwise help in the instruction of students with disabilities.

parental consent. Special education term used by IDEA that states that parents must have been fully informed in their preferred language or other mode of communication about all the information concerning the actions to which they are consenting and affirms that they understand and agree in writing to that action.

partially sighted. Condition in which an individual has a significant visual impairment but is able to capitalize on residual sight using magnification devices and other adaptive materials.

percentile rank, percentile. A score indicating the percentage of scores that occurs at or below a given score. A percentile rank of 75 means a score as high as or higher than 75 percent of all test takers.

performance-based assessment. Method of evaluation that measures what students can do with knowledge rather than measuring specific bits of knowledge the student possesses.

personal assistant, individual student aide. Paraprofessional specially trained to monitor and assist a particular student with a disability.

physical therapist, physical therapy (PT). Specialist with expertise in meeting students' needs in the area of gross motor skills. Provides consultation and support to staff to improve a student's educational performance related to functional gross motor development.

placement. Place where teaching will occur for a student with a disability.

portfolio assessment. Method of evaluation in which a purposeful collection of student work is used to determine student effort, progress, and achievement in one or more areas.

positive behavioral interventions and supports (PBIS). Strategies for preventing behavioral challenges and techniques for addressing common and intensive behavioral problems; PBIS is based on clearly defined outcomes, behavioral and biomedical science, research-validated practices, and systematic approaches.

positive reinforcement. Any stimulus or event that occurs after a behavior has been exhibited that increases the possibility of that behavior occurring in the future. A consequence to a behavior that causes it to increase. Also called a *reward.*

posttraumatic stress disorder (PTSD). A mental condition that results in a series of emotional and physical reactions in individuals who have either witnessed or experienced a traumatic event.

practice test. An accommodation used before students take tests. Students are given a test with the same format and content but different questions. Practice tests clarify test expectations and familiarize students with test content.

Present Levels of Academic Achievement and Functional Performance (PLAAFP) Information about a student's current level of academic achievement, social skills, behavioral communication skills, physical abilities and disabilities, and other areas that are included on an IEP or evaluation.

present level of functioning. Sometimes used informally during team meetings; an abbreviated reference to PLAAFP.

present level of performance (PLOP). The term previously used prior to being replaced by the more comprehensive PLAAFP.

preskill. Basic skill necessary for performing a more complex skill.

primary reinforcer. Food or other items related to human needs that cause a behavior to increase; used only occasionally in schools. An example of a primary reinforcer is a piece of candy earned for appropriate behavior.

private school. An option for some parents for their child's education. Students enrolled in private schools are eligible for assessments by the public (home) school district to determine if the student qualifies for special education. If he or she does qualify, the district of residence is responsible for writing an IEP.

probe. Quick and easy measure of student performance (accuracy and fluency) in the basic skills areas of reading, math, and written expression consisting of timed samples of academic behaviors.

program evaluation. An assessment decision concerning whether a special education program should be terminated, continued as is, or modified.

program placement. Type of assessment decision concerning where a student's special education services will take place.

progress monitoring assessments. Brief assessments given during the school year that inform teachers whether students are making adequate progress toward meeting grade-level performance benchmarks so support can be provided if they aren't.

progress on IEP objectives. An individualized grading accommodation in which a student's grade is based on the measurable goals and objectives and progress monitoring components of the IEP.

prompts. Assistance provided to a student in the form of suggesting or saying the next words of something forgotten.

psychological tests. Tests designed to measure how efficiently students learn in an instructional situation; often used to assess intelligence and to determine whether learning disabilities exist.

Public Law 94-142. Education for All Handicapped Children Act; first federal special education law that incorporated many of the rights captured today in IDEA.

push-in model. Specialists work closely with students in the general education classroom. Instructional support, differentiated instruction, or related services are provided in the classroom.

push-out model. Specialists work closely with students who need special education services outside the general education classroom once or more each day. Instructional support or related services are provided in small groups or one-on-one in a separate setting.

receptive language. An individual's ability to understand what people mean when they speak.

regular class. The primary placement for students without disabilities. Also referred to as a *general education class.*

reinforcement. Any response or consequence that causes a behavior to increase.

related services. Services provided to students with disabilities to enhance their ability to learn and function in the least restrictive environment (LRE). Such services may include in-school nursing and speech and language services. Services students with disabilities need to benefit from their educational experience. Examples of related services include transportation, speech therapy, physical therapy (PT), and counseling.

residential and private placements. A district may determine that a student requires residential or private placement services to provide free appropriate public education (FAPE) within an IEP. If determined by the district, the cost is borne by the district; if the placement is the choice of the parent, the parent bears the cost if the school district made FAPE available.

residential facility. Placement for students with disabilities when their needs cannot be met at a public school. Students attend school and live at a residential facility.

resource room. Setting in which a special education teacher works with groups of students with disabilities for parts of the school day.

resource specialist. Provides instructional planning and support and direct services to students whose needs have been identified in an IEP and are assigned to general education classrooms for the majority of their school day.

resource specialist program (RSP). Term used to describe a program that provides instruction, materials, and support services to students with identified disabilities who are assigned to general classroom for more than 50 percent of their school day.

resource teacher. Special education teacher who provides direct services to students with disabilities in a special education or general education classroom and who meets with teachers to solve the students' problems. Most often, resource teachers work with students with high-incidence disabilities.

response to intervention (RtI). An approach to the identification of learning disabilities based on whether student learning progress improves or fails to improve after the student receives increasingly intense, research-based interventions; the latter may be an indication of learning issues. A three-tiered model established under IDEA 2004 as an alternative to the discrepancy model for determining whether a student has a learning disability (LD).

school nurse. Specialist who has education, training, professional nursing licensure, and other required credentials who provides expertise in understanding and responding to students' medical needs, protects and promotes student health, facilitates optimal development, and advances academic success. Often serves as a liaison between medical and school professionals.

school nurse services. School health services that contribute to the goals of the educational and health care system by providing screenings and referrals, administering medications and treatments, providing first aid, providing health counseling and education, and supporting students to acquire self-management skills. IEP school nurse services are a related service (§1401(26)) and as such should be listed in the child's IEP (§1414(d)(1)(A)).

school psychologist. Specialist with expertise in assessing students' cognitive, academic, social, emotional, and behavioral domains. This professional also designs strategies to address students' academic and social behavior problems. Assists in the identification of students' intellectual, social, and emotional needs. School psychologists provide consultation and support to families and staff regarding student behavior and conditions related to learning. They plan programs to meet the special needs of children and often serve as facilitators during IEP meetings.

screening. In education, the process of examining groups of students to identify students at risk of school failure. In the public health model, it is a form of secondary prevention, i.e., finding those with some signs of a disease or disability to further identify the condition and provide ameliorative treatment if possible. See also *universal screening*.

Section 504. The section of the Rehabilitation Act of 1973 that prohibits discrimination against all individuals with disabilities in programs that receive federal funds.

self-advocacy. Extent to which a student can identify supports needed to succeed and communicate that information effectively to others including teachers and employers.

sensory processing disorder (SPD). A complex brain disorder that causes a child to misinterpret everyday sensory information such as movement, sound, or touch. Children with SPD may seek out intense sensory experiences or feel overwhelmed with information.

SMART goals. Goals that are specific, measurable, attainable, realistic/relevant, and time bound.

special day class. A self-contained special education class that provides services to students with intensive needs that cannot be met by the general education program. Classes consist of more than 50 percent of the student's day.

specialized instructional support personnel (SISP). Term in the federal ESSA (Every Student Succeeds Act) to describe personnel who provide professional services such as school nurses, school social workers, school psychologists, school counselors, speech-language pathologists or therapists, or occupational therapy (OT) or physical therapy (PT) providers.

specific learning disability (SLD). Special education term used to define a disorder in one or more of the basic psychological processes involved in understanding or using spoken or written language that may manifest itself in an imperfect ability to listen, think, speak, read, write, spell, or do mathematical equations including conditions such as perceptual disabilities, brain injury, minimal brain dysfunction, dyslexia, and developmental aphasia. Specific learning disabilities do not include learning problems that are primarily the result of visual, hearing, or motor disabilities, mental retardation, emotional disturbance (ED),, or of environmental, cultural, or economic disadvantage.

speech and language impairments. Communication disorders such as stuttering, impaired articulation, or language or voice impairment that adversely affect a child's educational performance.

speech and language specialist. Assesses students for possible delayed speech and language skills and provides direct services in the areas of phonology, morphology, syntax, semantics, and pragmatics. They are also available regarding hearing impairments and amplification.

standardized tests. Tests that compare the performance of each student with a representative group of students who take the same test using detailed procedures for administration, timing, scoring, and interpretation procedures that must be followed precisely to obtain valid and reliable results.

supplementary aids and services. IDEA term for a range of supports provided in general education classes and other education-related settings that enable students with disabilities to be educated with students who are not disabled to the maximum extent appropriate.

team teaching. Coteaching option in which students remain in one large group and teachers share leadership in the instructional activity of the classroom.

test administration. The conditions under which a test is given to students.

three-year reevaluation. Triannual process of reassessing the needs of a student with a disability carried out be a multidisciplinary team.

tier 1 instruction. Instruction in RtI that is evidence based and provided to all students in a class.

tier 2 instruction. Instruction in RtI provided in tier 1 plus additional small-group sessions that provided extra practice of targeted skills and content covered in tier 1.

tier 3 instruction. Instruction in RtI that consists of highly intensive instruction matched to the individual needs of students who continue to struggle despite well delivered, evidence-based instruction in tier 2.

time-out. Type of removal punishment in which a student is removed from opportunities for reward. An example of time out is a "penalty box" for misbehavior on the playground.

time sampling. Strategy for recording behavior in which a behavior is periodically observed and measured during a specified time.

token economy. Group behavior management procedure in which students earn a representative or token currency for appropriate behavior that can later be exchanged for rewards.

transition IEP. See individualized transition plan (ITP)."

transition specialist. Special educator who helps prepare students with disabilities for postschool activities including employment, vocational training, or higher education.

traumatic brain injury (TBI). Condition in which an individual experiences a significant trauma to the head from an accident, illness, or injury and that affects learning. TBI applies to open or closed head injuries resulting in impairment in one or more areas such as cognition; language; memory; attention; reasoning; abstract thinking; judgment; problem-solving; sensory, perceptual, and motor abilities; psychosocial behavior; physical functions; information processing; and speech. TBI does not apply to congenital or degenerative brain injuries or brain injuries induced by birth trauma.

tutorial. Computer program designed to present new material to students in small sequential steps and/or to review concepts.

universal screening. The process used in response to intervention (RtI) to assess all students to identify those who are having difficulty learning despite evidence-based tier 1 instruction.

video self-modeling. A form of instruction in which students learn by watching themselves successfully perform a behavior.

visual impairments. Condition in which an individual experiences a significant trauma to the head from an accident, illness, or injury that affects learning. Impairment in vision that even with correction adversely affects a child's educational performance. The term includes partial sight and blindness.

visual perceptual/visual motor deficit. A disorder that affects the understanding of information a person sees or the ability to draw or copy. A characteristic seen in people with learning disabilities such as dysgraphia or nonverbal LD. It can result in missing subtle differences in shapes or printed letters, losing place frequently, struggles with cutting, holding pencil too tightly, or poor eye/hand coordination.

vision specialist. Provides consultation and support to staff and direct instructional support to students with visual impairments. Provides functional vision assessments and curriculum modifications including Braille, large type, and aural media.

workability programs. Programs that focus on preparing high school students with disabilities for successful transition to employment, continuing education, and quality adult life with an emphasis on work-based learning opportunities.

written language difficulties. Problems that students with learning and behavioral disabilities have with skills related to handwriting, spelling, and written expression.

BIBLIOGRAPHY

American Academy of Child and Adolescent Psychiatry. 2014. "Attachment Disorders." January. Accessed December 2, 2018. https://www.aacap.org/aacap/families_and_youth/facts_for_families/fff-guide/Attachment-Disorders-085.aspx.

American Nurses Association and National Association of School Nurses. 2017. *School nursing: Scope and standards of practice.* 3rd ed. Silver Spring, MD: ANA & NASN.

American Psychiatric Association. 2013. *Diagnostic and Statistical Manual of Mental Disorders.* 5th ed. Arlington, VA: American Psychiatric Association.

"Assessment and Diagnosis." ADHD Institute (website) January 2017. Accessed December 2, 2018. https://adhd-institute.com/assessment-diagnosis/.

"Attention-Deficit/Hyperactivity Disorder (ADHD)." Centers for Disease Control and Prevention. 2018. Accessed December 2, 2018. https://www.cdc.gov/ncbddd/adhd/diagnosis.html.

AZQuotes.com. n.d. "Florence Nightingale." Accessed February 25, 2019. https://www.azquotes.com/author/10825-Florence_Nightingale.

Bateman, B., and C. Herr. 2006. *Writing measurable IEP goals and objectives.* 2nd ed. Verona, WI: Attainment Co.

Bateman, B., and Mary Anne Linden. 2006. *Better IEPs.* 4th ed. Verona, WI: Attainment Co.

Cedar Rapids Community School District v. Garret F., 119 S. Ct. 992,29 IDELR 966 (1999).

Children and Adults with Attention-Deficit/Hyperactivity Disorder (CHADD). 2018. "Understanding ADHD." *CHADD.* Accessed December 1, 2018. https://chadd.org/understanding-adhd/.

Cohen, Matthew. 2009. *A Guide to Special Education Advocacy: What Parents, Clinicians and Advocates Need to Know.* 1st ed. London and Philadelphia: Jessica Kinsley.

Collier, Idolia, Katheryn McCash, and Joanne Bartrann. 1996. *Writing Nursing Diagnoses.* New York, NY: Mosby.

Council for Exceptional Children. 1997. *Special Education in the Schools: CEC Policy Manual.* Accessed December 2, 2018. https://www.cec.sped.org/Policy-and-Advocacy/CEC-Professional-Policies/Special-Education-in-the-Schools.

Dawson, Peg, and R. Guare. 2009. *Executive Skills in Children and Adolescents.* New York: Guilford Press.

Deanze College, Faculty. 2017. "Nursing Diagnosis." *NANDA-approved nursing diagnoses 2018–2020.* August. Accessed December 2, 2018. https://www.deanza.edu/faculty/hrycykcatherine/Latest%20NANDA%20List.pdf.

Friend, Marilyn. 2016. *What's New in Special Education?* 5th ed. Upper Saddle River, NJ: Pearson Publishing.

Gelfmn, M. H. B., and N. Schwab, eds. 2001. "IDEA: Current Issues in Dispute." In *Legal Issues in School Health Services.* North Branch, MN: Sunrise River Press, 398–418.

Gibbons, L. J., K. Lehr, and J. Selekman. 2013. "Federal laws protecting children and youth with disabilities in the schools." In *School Nursing: A Comprehensive Text,* edited by J. Selekman. Philadelphia: F.A. Davis, 257–83.

Gordon, Marjory. 1982. *Nursing Diagnosis.* New York: McGraw-Hill.

Groom, Winston. 1986. *Forrest Gump.* New York: Doubleday.

Heward, W. L. 2017. *Exceptional Children: An Introduction to Special Education.* 11th ed. Boston: Pearson.

Illinois State Board of Education. "Developing Meaningful IEPs." August 2015. Accessed December 2, 2018. https://www.isbe.net/Documents/IEPs-with-NILS-pres141208.pdf.

_________. Every Student Succeeds Act (ESSA). 2018. Accessed December 2, 2018. https://www.isbe.net/Pages/ESSA.aspx.

_________. 2016. "Proposed Special Education." Accessed December 2, 2018. https://www.isbe.net/Documents/226ark.pdf#search=Special%2OEducation.

Irving Independent School District v. Tatro, 468 S. Ct. 833 (1984).

Jewish Women's Archive. (website) n.d. "Women of Valor: Lillian Wald." Brookline, MA. Accessed March 31, 2019 https://jwa.org/womenofvalor/wald.

Johns, Beverley H. 2016. *Your Classroom Guide to Special Education Law,* Baltimore: Brooks Publishing.

Kirk, S., J. Galleger, and M. Coleman. 2012. *Education Exceptional Children.* 13th ed. Belmont, CA: Wadsworth Publishing.

Learning Disabilities of America. "About Us." History of LDA. Accessed 10/16/2018, https://ldaamerica.org/about-us/.

Lerner, Janet, and Beverly Johns. 2015. *Learning Disabilities and Related Disabilities.* 13th ed. Stamford, CT: Cengage Learning. Accessed June 2017. https://ldaamerica.org/types-of-learning-disabilities.

National Association of School Nurses. 2016. "Education, licensure, and certification of school nurses (Position Statement)." *NASN.* Accessed June 2016. https://www.nasn.org/nasn/advocacy/professional-practice-documents/position-statements/ps-education.

National Center for Education Statistics. n.d. "NCES." Accessed June 2017. https://nces.ed.gov/program/digest/current_tables.asp.

National Center for Learning Disabilities. 2018. *Individuals with Disabilities Education Act (IDEA).* Accessed December 2, 2018. https://www.ncld.org/archives/action-center/learn-the-law/individuals-with-disabilities-education-act-idea.

Nightingale, Florence. 1915. *Florence Nightingale to Her Nurse.* New York: Macmillan.
Pirangelo, R., and G. Giuliani. 2007. *Understanding, Developing, and Writing Effective IEPs.* California: Corwin Press.
Reitz, Stephanie. 2011. Associated Press, in NBCNews.com, March 29, 2011. "Dyslexic Governor Brings Learning Disabilities to Limelight." Accessed October 16, 2018. http://www.nbcnews.com/id/42325206/ns/health-health_care/t/dyslexic-governor-brings-learning-disability-limelight/#.W8ZLEvZFyUk.
Selekman, Janice. 2013. *School Nursing: A Comprehensive Text.* 2nd Ed. Philadelphia: F.A. Davis.
Shaywitz, S. 2004. *Overcoming Dyslexia.* New York: Alfred Knopf.
State of Washington, Office of the Superintendent of Public Instruction, 2019, Olympia. Accessed March 30, 2019. http://www.k12.wa.us/HealthFitness/Standards/HPE-K-12StandardsIntro.pdf.
Stone, Lynda, email message to authors, March 25, 2019.
Titler, M. G. "The Evidence for Evidence-Based Practice Implementation," chapter 7 in Hughes, R. G., editor. *Patient Safety and Quality: An Evidence-Based Handbook for Nurses.* Rockville, MD: Agency for Healthcare Research and Quality (US), 2008.
Twachtman-Cullen, Diane, and Jennifer Twachtman-Bassett. 2011. *The IEP from A to Z: How to Create Meaningful and Measurable Goals and Objectives.* 2nd ed. California: Jossey-Bass.
Understanding Special Education.com. 2016. "Special Education Terms and Definitions." *Understanding Special Education.* Accessed December 2, 2018. https://www.understandingspecialeducation.com/special-education-terms.html.
US Congress. Americans with Disabilities Act Amendment Act. Pub. L. 110-325. 42 U.S.C. 12102. (2008).
______. Americans with Disabilities Act of 1990, 42 U.S.C., 12101, 104 Stat. 327 (1990).
______. Education of All Handicapped Children Act, 20 U.S.C, Pub. L. No. 94-142, (1975).
______. Individuals with Disabilities in Education Act. Pub. L. 101-476, 104 Stat. 1142, (2004).
______. Individuals with Disabilities Education Improvement Act. Pub. L. No. 108-446, 118 Stat. 2647 (2004). Accessed December 2, 2018. https://www.congress.gov/congressional-record/2004/11/17/house-section/article/h9895-2?q=%7B%22search%22%3A%5B%22HR+1350+2004%22%5D%7D&r=1.
______. Rehabilitation Act of 1973, 87 Stat. 355 (1973).
US Department of Education. 2010. Free Appropriate Public Education for Students with Disabilities: Requirements Under Section 504 of the Rehabilitation Act of 1973. Accessed December 2, 2018. https://

www2.ed.gov/about/offices/list/ocr/docs/edlite-FAPE504.html.

______. 2018. *LAWS & GUIDANCE GENERAL Family Educational Rights and Privacy Act (FERPA).* March 1. Accessed December 2, 2018. https://www2.ed.gov/policy/gen/guid/fpco/ferpa/index.html.

________. Code of Federal Regulations. *34 C.F.R. sections 300–303 [Special education and related service for students, pre-school children, and infants and toddlers].* Accessed May 6, 2018. https://sites.ed.gov/idea/regs/b/a/

________. National Center for Education Statistics *Digest of Education Statistics.* Accessed March 31, 2019. https://www2.ed.gov/programs/osepidea/618-data/state-level-data-files/index.html.

________. Office of Civil Rights. 2010. "Free appropriate education for students with disabilities. Requirements under Section 504 of the Rehabilitation Act of 1973." https://www2.ed.gov/about/.

________. Office of Special Education and Rehabilitation Services. "Annual Report to Congress on the implementation of the Individuals with Disabilities Education Act, 1988–1998." Accessed March 31, 2019. https://www2.ed.gov/about/reports/annual/osep/index.html.

________. "Policy Letter: April 16, 2001 to Pinal County Arizona, Deputy County Attorney Linda L. Harant" (US Department of Education, April 16 2001). Accessed March 30, 2019. https://sites.ed.gov/idea/idea-files/policy-letter-april-16-2001-to-pinal-county-arizona-deputy-county-attorney-linda-l-harant/.

US Legal. 2018. *Age of Majority Law and Legal Definition.* Accessed December 2, 2018. https://definitions.uslegal.com/a/age-of-majority.

Wright, Peter. 2004. "Comments to change in IDEA 2004." Accessed October 12, 2016. http://www.wrightslaw.com

Wright, Peter, and P. Wright. 2010. *All About IEPs.* 1st ed. Hartfield, VA: Harbor House Law Press.

________. n.d. *Special Education Law.* 2nd ed. Hartfield, VA: Harbor House Law Press.

________. 2019. *Developing Your Child's IEP Present Levels, Goals and Services, Accommodations.* Hartfield, VA: Harbor House Law Press. Accessed March 30, 2019. https://www.wrightslaw.com/info/iep.develop.popup.resp1.htm.

APPENDIX 1

Disability Categories and Definitions

The following conditions have been identified by the US Department of Education as meeting its criteria of childhood disability that may result in the need for special education.

Autism: a developmental disability significantly affecting verbal and nonverbal communication and social interaction, generally evident before age three, that adversely affects a child's educational performance. Other characteristics often associated with autism are engagement in repetitive activities and stereotyped movements, resistance to environmental change or change in daily routines, and unusual responses to sensory experiences.

Deaf-blindness: concomitant hearing and visual impairments, the combination of which causes such severe communication and other developmental and educational needs that they cannot be accommodated in special education programs solely for children with deafness or children with blindness.

Deafness: a hearing impairment that is so severe that the child is impaired in processing linguistic information through hearing, with or without amplification, that adversely affects a child's educational performance.

Emotional disturbance (ED): a condition exhibiting one or more of the following characteristics over a long period of time and to a marked degree that adversely affects a child's educational performance:

- An inability to learn that cannot be explained by intellectual, sensory, or health factors.
- An inability to build or maintain satisfactory interpersonal relationships with peers and teachers.

- Inappropriate types of behavior or feelings under normal circumstances.
- A general pervasive mood of unhappiness or depression.
- A tendency to develop physical symptoms or fears associated with personal or school problems.

Emotional disturbance (ED) includes schizophrenia. The term does not apply to children who are socially maladjusted, unless it is determined that they have an emotional disturbance (ED).

Hearing impairment: an impairment in hearing, whether permanent or fluctuating, that adversely affects a child's educational performance but that is not included under the definition of deafness in this section.

Intellectual disability: Significantly sub-average general intellectual functioning, existing concurrently with deficits in adaptive behavior and manifested during the developmental period, that adversely affects a child's educational performance.

Multiple disabilities: concomitant impairments (such as mental retardation-blindness or mental retardation-orthopedic impairment), the combination of which causes such severe educational needs that they cannot be accommodated in special education programs solely for one of the impairments. Multiple disabilities does not include deaf-blindness.

Orthopedic impairment: a severe orthopedic impairment that adversely affects a child's educational performance. The term includes impairments caused by a congenital anomaly, impairments caused by disease (e.g., poliomyelitis, bone tuberculosis), and impairments from other causes (e.g., cerebral palsy, amputations, and fractures or burns that cause contractures).

Other health impairment: having limited strength, vitality, or alertness, including a heightened alertness to environmental stimuli, that results in limited alertness with respect to the educational environment, that is due to chronic or acute health problems such as asthma, attention deficit disorder (ADD) or attention deficit hyperactivity disorder (ADHD), diabetes, epilepsy, a heart condition, hemophilia, lead poisoning, leukemia, nephritis, rheumatic fever, sickle cell anemia, and Tourette's syndrome; and adversely affects a child's educational performance.

Specific learning disability (SLD)—General. SLD means a disorder in one or more of the basic psychological processes involved in understanding or in using language, spoken or written, that may manifest itself in the imperfect ability to listen, think, speak, read, write, spell, or to do mathematical calculations, including conditions such as perceptual disabilities, brain injury, minimal brain dysfunction, dyslexia, and developmental aphasia.

Disorders not included. SLD does not include learning problems that are primarily the result of visual, hearing, or motor disabilities, of mental retardation, of emotional disturbance (ED), or of environmental, cultural, or economic disadvantage.

Speech or language impairment means a communication disorder, such as stuttering, impaired articulation, a language impairment, or a voice impairment, that adversely affects a child's educational performance.

Traumatic brain injury (TBI) means an acquired injury to the brain caused by an external physical force, resulting in total or partial functional disability or psychosocial impairment, or both, that adversely affects a child's educational performance. TBI applies to open or closed head injuries resulting in impairments in one or more areas, such as cognition; language; memory; attention; reasoning; abstract thinking; judgment; problem-solving; sensory, perceptual, and motor abilities; psychosocial behavior; physical functions; information processing; and speech. TBI does not apply to brain injuries that are congenital or degenerative, or to brain injuries induced by birth trauma.

Visual impairment including blindness: an impairment in vision that, even with correction, adversely affects a child's educational performance. The term includes both partial sight and blindness.

In addition to the thirteen disabilities that may be ascribed to any child aged 3–21, Developmental Delay (DD) may be applied:

Developmental delay (DD): Children aged three through nine experiencing developmental delays. Child with a disability for children aged three through nine (or any subset of that age range, including ages three through five), may include a child—

> Who is experiencing developmental delays, as defined by the State and as measured by appropriate diagnostic instruments and procedures, in one or more of the following areas: Physical development, cognitive development, communication development, social or emotional development, or adaptive development; and
>
> Who, by reason thereof, needs special education and related services.

For children under age three: Infant or toddler with a disability: an individual under three years of age who needs early intervention services because the individual is experiencing developmental delays, as measured by appropriate diagnostic instruments and procedures in one or more of the areas of cognitive development, physical development, communication development, social or emotional development, and adaptive development; or has a diagnosed physical or mental condition that has a high probability of resulting in development delays

At-risk infant or toddler: an individual under three years of age who would be at risk of experiencing a substantial developmental delay if early intervention services were not provided. (US Congress 2004 [71FR46753, Aug. 14, 2006, as amended 72 FR 61306, Oct. 30, 2007])

APPENDIX 2

Examples of Accommodations Written on a Student's IEP

In this appendix, the authors offer some examples of accommodations and modifications that may be made for a student with a health issue. Use these examples as needed with the knowledge that each student's IEP plan must be written based on the individual issues the student is experiencing.

Attention Deficit Hyperactivity Disorder (ADHD)

- administration of medication during school time
- state where medication is located
- keep medication log
- able to seek quiet space if needed
- other accommodations based on the student's needs

Asthma

- administration of medication during school time
- state where medication is located
- keep medication log
- able to seek quiet space if needed
- modify level for recess, gym activities
- medication before gym activities
- medication after school activities
- carry water bottle as needed
- bathroom accommodations
- may take MDI before gym activities
- medical alert bracelets
- other accommodations based on the student's needs

Cancer

- able to have rest periods
- modify level for recess, gym activities
- need pass between classes
- carry water bottle
- bathroom accommodations
- extra snacks in school for energy
- extra books at home when needed
- medical alert bracelets
- other accommodations based on the student's needs

Cardiac condition

- rest periods
- needs pass between classes
- exemptions from all or some required physical fitness testing

- physical activity restrictions per physician orders/recommendations; problems with climbing stairs, needs elevator pass
- gym activities, gym tests monitoring, after-school activities
- carry water bottle
- bathroom accommodations
- extra snacks in school for energy
- medical alert bracelets
- other accommodations based on the student's needs

Diabetes

- administration of insulin during school time
- keep insulin medication log
- able to seek quiet space if needed
- exemptions from some or all required physical fitness testing
- physical activity restrictions per physician orders/recommendations
- modify level for recess, gym activities, after-school activities
- carry water bottle
- bathroom accommodations
- extra snacks in school for energy
- medical alert bracelets
- other accommodations based on the student's needs

Seizures disorders

- rest periods
- problems with climbing stairs, needs elevator pass
- exemptions from some or all required physical fitness testing
- physical activity restrictions per physician orders/recommendations
- carry water bottle
- bathroom accommodations
- extra snacks in school for energy
- medical alert bracelets
- other accommodations based on the student's needs

Sickle Cell Disease

- rest periods
- needs pass between classes
- problems with climbing stairs, needs elevator pass
- exemptions from some or all required physical fitness testing
- physical activity restrictions per physician orders/recommendations; gym activities, gym tests monitoring, after-school activities
- carry water bottle
- bathroom accommodations
- extra snacks in school for energy
- medical alert bracelets
- other accommodations based on the student's needs

APPENDIX 3

Code of Federal Regulations Related to Special Education

The school nurse or special education staff should maintain the practice of reviewing federal law (US Congress) as well as the regulations written by federal agencies, in this case, the US Department of Education. Appendix 3 lists some of the foundational requirements of the IEP accessed at US Department of Education March 31, 2019. The entire set of CFR, Title 34, Education particularly Section 300 and its subparts related to special education and related service for students, preschool children, and infants and toddlers is at https://sites.ed.gov/idea/regs/b/a/.

Individualized Education Programs

§300.320 Definition of individualized education program.

(a) General. As used in this part, the term individualized education program or IEP means a written statement for each child with a disability that is developed, reviewed, and revised in a meeting in accordance with §§300.320 through 300.324, and that must include—

(1) A statement of the child's present levels of academic achievement and functional performance, including—

(i) How the child's disability affects the child's involvement and progress in the general education curriculum (i.e., the same curriculum as for non-disabled children); or

(ii) For preschool children, as appropriate, how the disability affects the child's participation in appropriate activities;

(2)

(i) A statement of measurable annual goals, including academic and functional goals designed to—

(A) Meet the child's needs that result from the child's disability to enable the child to be involved in and make progress in the general education curriculum; and

(B) Meet each of the child's other educational needs that result from the child's disability;

(ii) For children with disabilities who take alternate assessments aligned to alternate achievement standards, a description of benchmarks or short-term objectives;

(3) A description of—

(i) How the child's progress toward meeting the annual goals described in paragraph (2) of this section will be measured; and

(ii) When periodic reports on the progress the child is making toward meeting the annual goals (such as through the use of quarterly or other periodic reports, concurrent with the issuance of report cards) will be provided;

(4) A statement of the special education and related services and supplementary aids and services, based on peer-reviewed research to the extent practicable, to be provided to the child, or on behalf of the child, and a statement of the program modifications or supports for school personnel that will be provided to enable the child—

(i) To advance appropriately toward attaining the annual goals;

(ii) To be involved in and make progress in the general education curriculum in accordance with paragraph (a)(1) of this section, and to participate in extracurricular and other nonacademic activities; and

(iii) To be educated and participate with other children with disabilities and non-disabled children in the activities described in this section;

(5) An explanation of the extent, if any, to which the child will not participate with non-disabled children in the regular class and in the activities described in paragraph (a)(4) of this section;

(6)

(i) A statement of any individual appropriate accommodations that are necessary to measure the academic from IDEA edu.gov.

(a) General. The public agency must ensure that the IEP Team for each child with a disability includes—

(1) The parents of the child;

(2) Not less than one regular education teacher of the child (if the child is, or may be,

participating in the regular education environment);

(3) Not less than one special education teacher of the child, or where appropriate, not less than one special education provider of the child;

(4) A representative of the public agency who—

(i) Is qualified to provide, or supervise the provision of, specially designed instruction to meet the unique needs of children with disabilities;

(ii) Is knowledgeable about the general education curriculum; and

(iii) Is knowledgeable about the availability of resources of the public agency.

(5) An individual who can interpret the instructional implications of evaluation results, who may be a member of the team described in paragraphs (a)(2) through (a)(6) of this section;

(6) At the discretion of the parent or the agency, other individuals who have knowledge or special expertise regarding the child, including related services personnel as appropriate; and

(7) Whenever appropriate, the child with a disability.

(b) Transition services participants.

And other based on the student's needs.

(US Department of Education, Code of Federal Regulations Title 34, accessed March 31, 2019. https://sites.ed.gov/idea/regs/b/a/)

INDEX

bold denotes photo

B

C

D

E

F

G

H

M

N

O

P

R

S

T

U

V

W

Printed in the United States
By Bookmasters